Victory over Violence

Martin Hengel

Victory over Violence

Jesus and the Revolutionists

Translated by
David E. Green

With an Introduction by
Robin Scroggs

FORTRESS PRESS   Philadelphia

This book is a translation of *Gewalt und Gewaltlosigkeit: Zur "politischen Theologie" in neutestamentlicher Zeit,* Number 118 in the series "Calwer Hefte zur Förderung biblischen Glaubens und christlichen Lebens," edited by Gerhard Hennig and published by Calwer Verlag, Stuttgart, in 1971. It is translated here by arrangement with the publisher.

Library of Congress Catalog Card Number 73-79035

ISBN 0-8006-0167-X

3732B73   Printed in U.S.A.   1-167

Contents

To my friends
Otto Betz
Friedrich Mildenberger
Peter Stuhlmacher

ABBREVIATIONS

EvKomm   *Evangelische Kommentare*

EvTh   *Evangelische Theologie*

MPL   Migne, *Patrologia latina*

NTS   *New Testament Studies*

ThLZ   *Theologische Literaturzeitung*

ThW   Gerhard Kittel (ed.), *Theologisches Wörterbuch zum Neuen Testament* (Stuttgart: Kohlhammer, 1933–   ).

VT   *Vetus Testamentum*

ZNW   *Zeitschrift für die Neutestamentliche Wissenschaft*

Introduction

by Robin Scroggs

In 1970 a book appeared in the United States entitled *When All Else Fails*.[1] Once one learns that it was published by a church publishing house and contains essays by theologians, the conclusion could be easily drawn that the book must deal with the necessity of ultimate reliance and trust in God during the storms and stresses of the believer's life. In point of fact, however, it is about the means necessary for societal improvement when recourse to orderly change has brought no results. That is, the book discusses the possibility of *Christian* participation in violent revolutions.

On the surface, *Victory over Violence: Jesus and the Revolutionists*, written by the German New Testament scholar Martin Hengel, might seem far removed from this problem in our troubled century. Its subject is the response of early Palestinian Judaism to foreign domination, a response that culminated in the unsuccessful revolutionary war in A.D. 66–70. The author is centrally concerned to show that on the question of violence the position of Jesus and the early Christians was radically different from that of the Zealots, the Jewish "liberation front" of the first century A.D. Despite the difference of centuries, however, Hengel clearly intends his book to speak to the contemporary situation, in which Christians are debating the possible use of violence in revolution. And this means that the proper perspective for evaluat-

1. Ed. by IDO-C (International Documentation on the Contemporary Church) (Philadelphia: Pilgrim Press, 1970).

ing his work is not first, or perhaps even primarily, a grounding in the times of Jesus, but in the causes for and rationales of the contemporary Christian debate. Our first question, however, must be: How is it that talk about revolution has arisen in the United States?

WHY THE DEBATE IN THE UNITED STATES?

This is a pertinent question to the average Christian in this country, for talk about revolution must appear to him at best unnecessary and at worst subversive both of Christianity and of the state. Seated in the midst of the most affluent and self-complacent society in U.S. history, he probably cannot comprehend any *need* for revolution. He is, comparatively, as well off as he has ever been. Furthermore, he clearly does not expect his government to exercise a morality that is consonant with his faith. The government's execution of the Vietnam War has not excessively troubled him, and the people's increased desire in the early 1970s to disengage seems to be based far more on a sense of exhaustion and purposelessness than on the constant and repeated personal and denominational declarations that the war is immoral and contradictory to Christian faith.

The resounding defeat of Senator McGovern in the 1972 presidential elections established "middle America's" (and therefore the average Christian's) rejection of any stance that seemed to it too left wing. Even labor, the traditional basis for support of the left, failed to rally solidly behind the Democratic candidate. According to post-election analysis, the only group that consistently supported him besides the academic community was the very poor and below-subsistence-level family.[2] And this means, *statistically speaking*, that there are not many poor people.

2. *The Chicago Daily News*, Nov. 9, 1972 (UPI release).

The subversiveness of the phrase "violent revolution" must seem frighteningly clear to church members who have been well educated to think of Christianity in terms of stability, status quo, and legality. Is not the Christian called to obedience to the state and to the avoidance of violence? His self-image, it is true, has been educated so that he can accept a role as soldier under the established government obeying all orders of the military, but it will not permit him the comparable role of a violent revolutionary prepared to kill in order to overthrow the government.

Yet despite this consensus within the mainstream church, some Christians have raised a banner of revolution under the names "theology of revolution" or "theology of liberation." Contrary to the views of the consensus, the need for change seems so pressing to the "Christian revolutionist" that he cannot understand the failure of others to see it. Blacks and other minority groups, racial or otherwise (e.g., the poor in Appalachia) are mostly frozen within very repressive structures. Government commitment to big business and the military seems to the revolutionist rigid and almost total, and as long as this commitment holds, he knows that money so desperately needed for the basic health and education of United States citizens will never be forthcoming. The effects of the government's commitment to the military-industrial complex can be seen both in the government's lukewarm attitude toward the ecological crisis as well as in the policy that it pursues in Vietnam. To the revolutionist the Vietnam holocaust is but the most recent, if the most tragic, example of U.S. imperialism, which consistently has put down attempts at genuine liberation within third world countries. (See, for example, the U.S. "invasion" of Santo Domingo in 1965.) Thus the United States seems to have become the prime symbol of anti-human repression in our times. The defeat of McGovern will only have underscored the revolutionist's already entrenched suspicion that orderly process of redress through courts, legislation, and elections is not a realistic hope. And his Christian ethical stance will not let him give up or become a quietist. He turns, therefore, to explore the potentialities in revolution. Where else can he go when all else has failed?

Discussion about revolution by U.S. Christians is an outgrowth of similar debates that have been going on in Europe, South America, and Africa. The Marxist-Christian dialogue has been proceeding apace for some years, and some Christians have become increasingly involved in actual revolutionary movements, particularly in South America. Much of Martin Hengel's work, including the present book, *Victory over Violence*, has its *locus* within the current European debate. That there *is* a debate implies, of course, disagreement, not only between those for and against revolution, but also among those who do agree that some kind of revolution is necessary. This disagreement arises over strategies and moral justifications, but above all over the question of the legitimacy of violence. Since it is to this key problem that *Victory over Violence* is devoted, it should prove useful here to sketch the various arguments that have been used to justify or reject Christian participation in violent revolution.

ARGUMENTS FOR AND AGAINST A VIOLENT REVOLUTION

First, *revolution* must be distinguished from *evolution*.[3] Evolution in this context can be defined as working within the structures for orderly change, hoping through enlightened legislators and legislation to make the necessary breakthrough

3. So Almeri Bezerra de Melo, "Revolution and Violence," *When All Else Fails*, p. 42. Where possible all footnotes in the Introduction refer to U.S. authors in order to provide the reader with a modest bibliography of current writings in this country. The present note is an exception (De Melo is from Brazil).

toward the requisite equality and freedom. This way largely characterizes the so-called old liberal approach. The revolutionist tends to view this approach as bankrupt and to heap scorn on the heads of the old liberals.[4] Liberalism is said to have failed, primarily because it has too benign a view of the structural flexibilities and too naïve a view of the power-holders within these structures.

The gravity of the crisis and the entrenched refusal of the establishment to deal positively with the crisis seem to the radical to call rather for revolution, which works from the outside to destroy the old structures and create new, more equitable ones. Here a further distinction between nonviolent and violent revolution needs to be made. In the United States minor nonviolent revolutions in the form of protests have been frequent during the last two decades and have received Christian approbation in certain, limited quarters. In the areas of racial segregation and the Vietnam war, these tactics have even perhaps had limited successes in provoking change. But for some Christian revolutionists these changes have been too few and sporadic to justify hope that nonviolence will be effective. Thus the lack of confidence in nonviolent methods leads them to consider the possibility that violence may become necessary.

For all concerned this is a disturbing consideration. Any believer who participates in violence can do so only after an agonizing assessment of the Christian faith and human need. The dilemma upon which the debate of nonviolent versus violent revolution revolves can be summed up in two questions. How can the Christian bring himself to commit violence and be true to his faith? How can the Christian refuse to use all means which will aid in relieving man's utter misery and

4. E.g., Richard Shaull, "A Theological Perspective on Human Liberation," in *When All Else Fails*, p. 56; James Cone, *Black Theology and Black Power* (New York: Seabury Press, 1969), pp. 26–28.

be true to his faith? This paradox eliminates certitude from either position, and the only possible stance is decisional and confessional. No matter how one decides, there is no relief from agony even after the decision, since no position eliminates the threat to full human existence.

How does the Christian contemplating violent revolution state his case?

He may argue that violence already exists in our society.[5] There is actual physical violence practiced by the police and national guard, a violence too easily glossed over because it is establishment, that is "authorized" violence. It hardly requires a liberal mentality to see that Blacks and radical students have been subjected to continual violence by various departments of government. Furthermore, nonphysical violence is just as real and often more destructive in our society than the overtly physical. The exclusion of Blacks from adequate job opportunities and the terrible and demeaning squalor the poor of whatever color are forced to endure are violence of the worst sort. Thus the question of violence becomes relativized. No longer is it a question of violence or not, but of *which* violence. Is not the violence accompanying a revolution justified if it brings to an end the violence practiced every day by the establishment?

He may argue that a nonviolent revolution is an impossible possibility.[6] The powers of government are so reactionary and strong that nonviolent postures will ultimately fail. If the Christian is serious about the overwhelming need for revolution, then he must accept the necessity of violence. Without violence there will be *no* revolution.

---

5. Cf. the helpful discussion in George Edwards, *Jesus and the Politics of Violence* (New York: Harper & Row, 1972), pp. 1–20.
6. Cf. George Celestin, "A Christian Looks at Revolution," in *New Theology No. 6*, ed. by Martin Marty and Dean Peerman (New York: Macmillan, 1969), p. 101.

He may appeal to past Christian support of the wars mounted by the government. He does not find it difficult factually to support his claim that the church in this country has, *de facto* at least, supported the wars of the government, without evaluating the moral position of the nation in the war. But if the church supports the violence of a war, how can it *a priori* deny the validity of a violent revolution?[7] Sometimes at this point the Christian acknowledges that the church *ought* to make moral judgments and be selective about which wars it should support. Some wars have just causes; others do not. In ethical discussions this has been called the just-war theory. At this point the advocate of violent revolution can respond: But if there is a just war, then there may also be such a thing as a just revolution.[8] Christian support throughout the centuries of war violence makes somewhat ludicrous the church's attempt to condemn all revolutions that resort to force.

He may resort to the position of situationalist ethics to support his acceptance of violence. That is, he can argue that Christian faith does not lay down a dogmatic set of ethical rules which are to be followed in all circumstances.[9] There are, it is admitted, statements within Christian tradition advocating nonviolence or even pacifism (however much ignored in times of war), including statements attributed to Jesus; but these were addressed to specific situations in the past and are not determinative of Christian action in the present. The contemporary Christian is faced with the responsibility of making his own decision about violence in view of the needs

7. De Melo, *When All Else Fails*, pp. 45–50.
8. Cf. the discussion in Edwards, *Jesus*, pp. 127–30. Also John Bennett, "Christian Responsibility in a Time that Calls for Revolutionary Change," in *Marxism and Radical Religion*, ed. by John Raines and Thomas Dean (Philadelphia: Temple University Press, 1970), pp. 66–68.
9. E.g., Cone, *Black Theology*, pp. 139–43.

of the times. In this perspective, a violent revolution against extreme repressive conditions has just as much claim to be "Christian" as a posture of nonviolence.

How does the advocate of nonviolent revolution reply to these arguments? It should be emphasized that he shares completely with the advocate of violence sensitivity to the desperate needs in society.[10] But there seems to be one basic difference in point of view that determines different approaches to the key issues. He may himself come close to the situationalist point of view in ethics, but he believes that there is at least *one* rule which does pertain to all situations. This rule is the love of neighbor (including the enemy), and this in his view excludes the use of force to cause harm to any person.[11] A Christian is called to protest and may even give up his own life in that protest, but to take another's life is *always* wrong, no matter how much alleviation of misery that killing might bring. He can fully admit the reality of establishment violence but denies that violence should meet violence. He may not be sanguine about the success of nonviolent revolutions (though appealing to Gandhi and Martin Luther King) but he denies that ends ever justify means. He may respond to the just war–just revolution argument by denying that there is moral justification (at least since atomic weapons) for any war and can then consistently reject the just revolution.[12] He may also lift up more realistically than the advocate of violence the pragmatic ambiguity of a violent revolution. Revolutions rarely succeed, and when they do,

10. A particularly illuminating description of the nonviolent revolutionist position is to be found in Arthur G. Gish, *The New Left and Christian Radicalism* (Grand Rapids, Mich.: Eerdmans, 1970).
11. For a strong statement see that of the German scholar, H. W. Bartsch, "The Foundation and Meaning of Christian Pacifism," in *New Theology*, pp. 185–98. Cf. also Gish, *New Left*, pp. 136–42.
12. So Martin Hengel himself, in *Was Jesus a Revolutionist* (Philadelphia: Fortress Press, 1971), p. 32, n. 87.

rather than ending violence, they tend to produce more violence, if in other forms. History does not lead one to be optimistic that *this* revolution will be the *last*.[13]

APPEAL TO THE BIBLE FOR SANCTIONS

Given the ambiguity of the situation, it is not surprising that advocates on both sides turn to the Christian tradition to find justifications for their views. Sadly enough, perhaps, the Christian past provides little support for either position, for mainstream Christianity has provided few models for revolutionary change.[14] But there is one source to which the revolutionist has turned for support, and this is the Bible. It is indeed surprising to see with what regularity the biblical basis for revolution is developed in recent writings on the subject; once more the Bible has become *the* source book for reformation and change, this time under the banner of human liberation. Since *Victory over Violence* directly deals with the biblical sanction, it may be useful to see just what kinds of support the revolutionist believes the Bible affords him.

The Bible (both Old and New Testaments) presents man with a view of the dynamic God who creatively leads his

---

13. Cf. Gish, *New Left,* pp. 139–42 and Edwards, *Jesus,* p. 122.
14. It should be stated, however, that recent literature about the fringe groups in Christian tradition has emphasized the revolutionary nature and the interest in social change of some of those groups. The interested reader should consult Michael Walzer, *The Revolution of the Saints* (Cambridge, Mass.: Harvard University Press, 1965); Norman Cohn, *The Pursuit of the Millennium* (New York: Oxford University Press, 1970); Rosemary Ruether, *The Radical Kingdom* (New York: Harper & Row, 1970); Gish, *New Left,* pp. 40–75; and the German author, Ernst Bloch, *Atheism in Christianity* (New York: Herder & Herder, 1972), who claims Augustine among others for the revolutionist's camp, as does also Richard Shaull, "Revolutionary Change in Theological Perspective," in *The Church Amid Revolution,* ed. by Harvey G. Cox (New York: Association Press, 1967), pp. 33–36.

people out of the past into the future.[15] This God is not to be identified with the status quo or the establishment; he is rather a God who desires creative change by his people. Thus when revolution leads to greater benefits to his people, God is a God of revolution, not of the establishment.

Biblical messianism, that is, the faith in the liberation of God's people on earth, has also become an important sanction.[16] Both in the Old and New Testaments, the actual historical and political order is taken seriously. God seeks to rule over this order and claims it for Himself and for righteousness. In this messianism there is thus both a condemnation of the demonic, repressive order, and a working toward a liberating and authentically human society. When the church proclaims Jesus to be Christ and Lord, it does so not primarily in the expectation of seeing him in a future heaven, but in confident hope that God has reclaimed the cosmos through his Christ and is subordinating it to his righteous demands. The revolution is thus a contribution to the realization of that divine claim over the world. Here a position is assumed not unlike that of the Zealots, which also took its messianism seriously.

The New Testament motif of death and resurrection can be presented as a model for action. For those espousing nonviolence, death is emphasized more than resurrection.[17] Just as did Jesus, the Christian must accept suffering as part of his obedience to God. The believer must stand with a theology of the cross, not a theology of glory, and that means he must

15. E.g., Shaull, *When All Else Fails*, pp. 53–58; Cone, *Black Theology*, pp. 64 f.; Roland Smith, "A Theology of Rebellion," in *New Theology*, pp. 137 f.
16. E.g., Shaull, *When All Else Fails*, pp. 55 f. and the same author in Carl Oglesby and Richard Shaull, *Containment and Change* (New York: Macmillan, 1967), pp. 216–27; Cone, *Black Theology*, pp. 121–27; Celestin, *New Theology*, p. 101; J. Christian Beker, "Biblical Theology Today," in *New Theology*, pp. 31 f.
17. Cf. Edwards, *Jesus*, pp. 97 f.; Gish, *New Left*, p. 141.

be prepared to resign all claim upon and expectation from the world. He witnesses to the reality of love but is not permitted to expect that witness to lead to success. For those considering violence the emphasis is somewhat changed. The believer must be prepared, as a good revolutionary, to die for his cause; only through the violence of death will the new society, symbolized by the resurrection, emerge.[18]

No appeal to the Bible, however, can ignore Jesus, his mission and message—and the battle to claim him for both violent and nonviolent revolutions has become increasingly shrill in recent years. This is a crucial battle for those whose faith credits Jesus as the authoritative sanction. Whatever Jesus taught about violence decides the issues. Even for those, however, who would see Jesus as an example (among others) but not as a unique sanction, he is important. Jesus may be only an example, but he cannot help but be one of the most important examples. We have here moved to the center of Christian faith and are at the place where we can turn to the thesis of *Victory over Violence.*

JESUS AND THE ZEALOTS

Much of the work of Martin Hengel has been directed to the study of the Zealots, a Jewish religious-political sect of the first century A.D., and the possible relationships Jesus and early Christianity may have had with this revolutionary group. On the surface any relation between Jesus and the Zealots would seem incredible. The Zealots were, at least in the extreme wing, a terrorist group that sanctioned violence both against the Romans and Jewish collaborationists. The Gospels present a Jesus who proclaims a pacifistic and loving stance toward all men, friends or enemies. The New Testa-

18. Shaull, *When All Else Fails*, pp. 58 f.; Cone, *Black Theology*, pp. 64 f.

ment writings, furthermore, all but ignore the Zealots, although during the time of the formation of many of these documents, the Zealotic question was a burning issue in Palestine.

The ferment of our times, however, has made inevitable the attempt to find a prototype in Jesus for social change, and one result has been the recent popularization of previous attempts to link Jesus closely with the major revolutionary movement of his day.[19] In an earlier work, Hengel examined this possibility and came to the conclusion that the arguments are not defensible.[20] While Jesus held certain interests and concerns in common with the Zealots, the freedom he proclaimed was essentially an inner, nonpolitical freedom, and he opposed violence to any group of people. Jesus' message was above the party concerns of any specific sector of society.

In the present work, Hengel advances his argument an important stage further. Here he puts the stance of Jesus and the early Christians squarely within the political and societal setting of the first century. He sketches vividly the oppressive policies of the successive foreign rulers of Palestine and shows how the Jewish resistance movement originated and fanned the fires of yearning for political freedom. He argues that this resistance movement was primarily motivated by religious concerns and yet that the success of the revolt

19. The major work in question is S. G. F. Brandon, *Jesus and the Zealots* (New York: Charles Scribner's Sons, 1967), a careful and detailed scholarly statement. The problem is that to reach his conclusions the author has to stretch his evidence beyond all reasonable limits and to argue that the Gospels have suppressed other evidence because of their concern to present a pacifistic Jesus. The argument from silence involved here has to bear more weight than is allowable.
20. *Was Jesus a Revolutionist?* In two as-yet-untranslated works Hengel lays the groundwork for his present conclusions. The first was a masterful study of the Zealots, *Die Zeloten* (Leiden: Brill, 1961); the second, a study of Jesus in which he places him more within the charismatic than the political camp, *Nachfolge und Charisma* (Berlin: Töpelmann, 1968).

against the Greek oppressors ultimately led to a Jewish rule as politically and militarily oppressive as the foreign rule it replaced.

The return to foreign control under the Romans (albeit in part indirectly through the Herodian family) exchanged bad conditions for worse, argues Hengel, and the resurgence of the resistance movement in the first century A.D. was thus almost inevitable. He traces the explicit emergence of the Zealotic party back to the early years of that century and attempts to show that increasing Roman oppression was countered by increasing violent resistance, counterforces that culminated in the national revolt against Rome in A.D. 66–70. It is into this almost Hegelian thesis-antithesis view of historical movement that Hengel places Jesus and documents the clear distinction between the Zealotic program and Jesus' own position.

This picture of the political setting of Jesus' time is by no means simply designed to fill gaps in the reader's knowledge of first-century Palestine; it has a function in the contemporary debate. Hengel is himself opposed to the appropriation of violence by the Christian; he believes neither in the just war nor the just revolution. In his previous work he demonstrated, to most scholars' satisfaction I believe, that Jesus rejected the use of force, and Hengel's implicit conclusion is that the twentieth-century believer should follow suit. But the argument can be raised at this point that simply to base a contemporary stand on what Jesus said two thousand years ago is not valid. In that case Jesus' words would have become an abstract ideal, or even a law. No, the appeal to Jesus must be more sophisticated than that. In many scholarly circles today the point is continually made, and with justice, that Jesus spoke to a concrete situation and his teaching cannot be abstracted from that situation. In this view the words of Jesus should not be taken as literally applicable to the present scene, *unless the scene is similar or analogous to that scene which Jesus addressed.*

The sketch which Hengel draws in this book is clearly designed to show that our current situation, which for some requires a revolutionary solution, is very much like that in first-century Palestine. He speaks of the "monstrous extent of oppression and exploitation, violence and counterviolence in Jewish Palestine in the time of Jesus" (p. 64). He claims that "the injustice and suffering in Palestine two thousand years ago was certainly no less than the suffering in our world today" (p. 57). Thus Jesus *did* confront a world similar to ours. He did see military, economic, and social oppression and violence just as we see today. He too was horrified by this inhumanity to man. Likewise, the revolutionary option was available to him as it is today. He could have joined forces with the Zealots and argued that the situation was too hopeless for anything but a violent revolution to meet successfully. Jesus, however, rejected that possibility, chose a radically different course which was above the violence both of repression and revolution. Since Jesus, faced with a situation similar to that of contemporary man, rejected violence, so must the believer today "take seriously the radically different response of Jesus" (p. 64).

Hengel's ultimate conclusion thus rests on three claims. First, Jesus rejected the Zealotic option. Secondly, the political-economic scene in first-century Palestine was singularly desperate. Thirdly, an appeal to Jesus' teaching, given the analogous situation, is appeal to an authority which should guide contemporary decisions. The first two of these claims rest on assessment of historical data; the third, on theological premises. The reader should be alert to these claims and to some of the problems and issues involved in making them.

That Jesus rejected the Zealotic option is more assumed

than argued in this book, and the reader is referred to Hengel's earlier publication, *Was Jesus a Revolutionist?*, where the issue is discussed in some detail. It would be my judgment that most researchers would agree with the basic conclusion Hengel reaches in that publication. Many scholars would also agree that there was great unrest among Palestinian Jews at this time, an unrest that found expression in Zealotic and other messianic movements. Nevertheless, the evidence for such unrest is surprisingly scanty, and it is legitimate at least to raise the question whether first-century Judaism would be seen as so messianic-conscious were it not for the interest displayed by the New Testament in the messianic question. Josephus, the main historical source for this period, says little that would suggest rampant unrest during Jesus' lifetime; thus Hengel is forced to take refuge in the argument (used by others before him) that as a patron of the Roman government, Josephus played down Roman oppression and Jewish antagonism. It is not entirely clear that there was adequate cause for unrest, that Roman government was harsher than that of previous overlords, that Roman taxation was more exorbitant than that of other times (including our own), that the average Jewish peasant felt the hand of Rome in an especially heavy manner, or even that the peasant particularly cared to whom he paid his taxes. Thus there might be room for disagreement with the assertion that the scene for Palestinian Jews at that time was as desperate and hopeless as it is for people in South America, Africa, or even for the Blacks and poverty-stricken people in North America.

The third claim, that Jesus' stand is authoritative for the believer today, is stated with circumspection. The theological premises are complex, and the reader should understand that not all theological positions within Christianity would find an appeal to the historical Jesus necessary (or even possible!). Hengel does not discuss the options or say in what sense he would claim Jesus to be authoritative. He simply calls attention to Jesus as a possible sanction and invites the reader's response. He has, as we have seen, protected himself against the charge that he has lifted Jesus' teaching out of the concrete context of his time. In fact, one of the genuine joys of the book is that in it Jesus takes on sharper focus because he is viewed within the turbulence of his day and his own views are clarified because they are seen as the result of a struggle for a stance different from other options open to his society. Hengel's work is a model of how the historical Jesus ought to be presented to modern man.

How, then, does *Victory over Violence* contribute to the contemporary debate in this country? In concluding that Jesus "demanded renunciation of violence and love of enemies" (p. 49), the book holds up Jesus as a model of nonviolence. Since this model should be a crucial sanction for Christians, it suggests that the believer today must reject the option of the violent revolution. It claims that true freedom is first and foremost inner freedom, a freedom from sin (including aggressive instincts) and for service. It implies that success is subordinate to principle; the issue is not what will happen if the revolution fails, but what sort of actions I can perform that are consonant with Jesus' ethic of love. Even a situationalist ethic, from Hengel's perspective, would be judged not primarily from the standpoint of its success in achieving all that the neighbor needs, but in its fidelity to the model of nonviolent love. Seen thus, *Victory over Violence* is very much to the point in the United States and should take its place as a major contribution to Christian reflection upon this most serious and agonizing problem of our day.

Author's Preface

The short study here presented is a selective summary of a much more extensive work on the subject of imperialism, messianic war, and nonviolence, whose completion has been delayed by pressures of time. This more extensive work is based in turn on a lecture before the exegetical study group on the problems of peace sponsored by the Evangelical Student Association at Heidelberg. My purpose is to take up the themes already introduced in *Was Jesus a Revolutionist?* (Philadelphia: Fortress Press, 1971) and expand on them within a wider historical setting. It is striking to see how little attention the assertions of today's "political theology" or "theology of revolution" pay to the political situation of Jesus and primitive Christianity, and how little use is made for the response given by the New Testament to the political demands of its age. This study is intended to bridge this gap and encourage the reader to study the sources on his own. For this reason detailed citations have been included.

The work concentrates deliberately on the problem of violence, today the center of so much debate, to which the New Testament itself gives a clear and unequivocal response that Christian social ethics cannot evade if it is to remain true to its own nature. It is my particular hope that this investigation might contribute to an intensification of the dialogue, hitherto only sporadic, between New Testament theology and Christian social ethics.

I should like to express my thanks to my assistant Knoll for several bibliographical references, and to my assistants Mer-

kel and Müller for their criticism of the manuscript and help
with the proofreading.

Erlangen, Easter, 1971   Martin Hengel

Introduction

Despite the dubious past of "political theology," this attractive concept has once more become the focus of considerable attention.[1] To the ancient world—to the Jews as to the Greeks—the notion was taken for granted; it could almost be called banal. To men of that period theology and politics were not two fundamentally separate domains to be united by dint of laborious effort; they were instead intimately allied, in fact identical. The Torah, which God had given to Israel at Sinai, contained the necessary directives for the proper organization of the nation, down to the laws governing the king and rules for the conduct of war (Deut. 17:14–20; 20:1–20). The Hellenistic kings and their heirs, the Roman Caesars, appeared as manifestations of the deity and enjoyed cultic veneration. Even while still alive they were worshiped as superhuman "saviors" (*sōterēs*) of their subjects. In other words, the religions of the ancient world were by definition—

1. On the history of this term, see Ernst Feil, " 'Politische Theologie' und 'Theologie der Revolution,' " in Ernst Feil and Rudolf Weth, eds., *Diskussion zur "Theologie der Revolution"* (München: Kaiser, 1969). Important critical reservations have been expressed by Hans Maier, " 'Politische Theologie'? Einwände eines Laien," in Helmut Peukert, ed., *Diskussion zur "politischen Theologie"* (Mainz: Matthias-Grünewald, 1969), pp. 1–25; see also the bibliography *ibid.*, pp. 302 ff. In the past forty years the term has apparently undergone a complete transformation. Carl Schmitt, a conservative student of constitutional law and legal theoretician of national socialism, entitled one of his works *Politische Theologie* (München: Duncker & Humblot, 1922; 2nd ed., 1934). On the fundamental parallels between his theory of the state and that of the extreme left, above all H. M. Enzensberger, see Hans Matthias Kepplinger, *Rechte Leute von Links* (Olten: Walter, 1970), *passim*.

as it is so well put today—"politically relevant," and politics always had to be understood as a religious function. The proper working of the state was indissolubly linked with the favor of the gods who established and maintained nations and cities.[2]

Among the revolutionary effects of Jesus and primitive Christianity was the disruption of this "naïve unity" of religion and politics. The numinous glow of political power and its exercise was relativized, demythologized, and thus "emptied of power."[3]

In the study that follows I should like to attempt, by way of illustration, to trace one line of historical development out of this very complex series of events. I shall deal with the Jewish reaction to Hellenistic and later Roman imperialism, a reaction that was in large measure religiously motivated, but at the same time had very concrete political consequences, which were expressed both in the apocalyptic ideology of the messianic holy war and in a long series of bloody rebellions. One could speak of a Jewish "theology of revolution" unique in the ancient world, developed not only in learned apocalyptic literature but also in relentless "revolutionary practice." The message of Jesus and the primitive Christian community stands in radical opposition to this apocalyptic Jewish "theology of revolution," and yet from the religio-historical point

2. It is no accident that the term "political theology" goes back to Hellenistic philosophy; see Feil, " 'Politische Theologie'," pp. 114–15, and Martin Persson Nilsson, *Geschichte der griechischen Religion* (2nd ed.; München: Beck, 1955–1961), vol. 2, pp. 282 ff. For Israel, see Otto Michel in *Neutestamentliche Studien für Rudolf Bultmann* ("Beihefte zur Zeitschrift für die Neutestamentlich Wissenschaft," 21 [Berlin: Töpelmann, 1954]), p. 66: "But for Israel the goal of religious faith is always political, and the political goal is determined by religious faith."
3. See note 105. On this point there is agreement even between such totally different statements as John 18:36 ("My kingdom does not belong to this world") and the bluntly anti-Roman visions of Revelation 13 and 17.

of view is dependent on this theology at several essential points. Both Jesus and the Jewish apocalyptic writers contrasted the imminent sovereignty of God to the unrighteousness of the historical present; but there was a radical difference in the manner in which they expected God to impose his sovereign authority. To develop a "political theology" today it will be all-important to work out this dialectic of tension between the preaching of Jesus and the expectations of his Jewish environment.

Macedonia and   II

Greek Imperialism

The great turning point that fundamentally altered the ancient world was the Persian campaign of Alexander.[4] In 334 B.C. a twenty-two-year-old leader set out with a small army of barely thirty-five thousand men to destroy the Persian Empire and penetrate as far as India. He thus demonstrated unsurpassably to the eastern nations the absolute technological and rational superiority of the new rulers of the world, the Macedonians and Greeks. Tyre, the invulnerable coastal fortification of the Phoenicians, which Nebuchadnezzar had besieged for thirteen years without success two hundred fifty years before, fell into his hands after a siege of seven months unparalleled in the history of ancient warfare. The Philistine city of Gaza and—after an attempted rebellion—Samaria also, two rivals of Jerusalem, were destroyed, their population executed in part, in part sold into slavery. The king settled Macedonian military colonists in Samaria. The apocalypse of Isaiah (Isaiah 24—27) probably reflects this destruction of the enemy city, while Zech. 9:1–8 refers to the threatened judgment against Tyre and Gaza. But this means that the political cataclysm wrought by Alexander's campaign also

4. William Woodthorpe Tarn, *Alexander the Great* (New York: Cambridge University Press, 1948–1950 [2nd ed. of vol. 1, 1951]), vol. 1, pp. 10 ff., 40 ff.; Hermann Bengtson, *Griechische Geschichte von den Anfängen bis die römische Kaiserzeit* ("Handbuch der Altertumswissenschaft," 3. Abt., 4. Teil [3rd ed.; München: Beck, 1965]), pp. 326 ff. Cf. G. Wirth in *Chiron*, 1 (1971), pp. 135–52.

made a deep impression on the tiny Jewish nation, stimulating apocalyptic prophecy.[5] One hundred sixty years later, in the apocalypse of Daniel, Alexander still inaugurates the final epoch of world history. The Macedonian-Greek Empire established by him is superior to all earlier empires:

> Then I saw a fourth beast, dreadful and grisly, exceedingly strong, with great iron teeth and bronze claws. It crunched and devoured, and trampled underfoot all that was left. It differed from all the beasts which preceded it.   (Dan. 7:7)[6]

The final fourth empire thus symbolized surpasses all the other empires of the world not only in its destructive might but also in its abysmal wickedness. It therefore appears as the culmination of human hubris and violence preceding the irruption of the kingdom of God, which spells an end to human history. But the apt characterization of Alexander and his Diadochi—military might, merciless exploitation of the subject nations, and self-deification of the ruler—could also be applied in the eyes of the Jewish observer to the governmental authority of the Romans without qualification; it is therefore only too easy to see why Daniel's final, fourth empire was identified with Rome, which was looked upon as the "wicked empire" (*malkût ṣādôn*).[7] This highly negative picture of Macedonian and Greek hegemony among the Jews stands in fundamental contrast to the relatively positive light in which the Persian Empire appears, although here, too, differences can be noted.[8]

5. Martin Hengel, *Judentum und Hellenismus* ("Wissenschaftliche Untersuchungen zum Neuen Testament," 10 [Tübingen: Mohr, 1969]), pp. 22 ff., 31.
6. Cf. Dan. 2:40 and the introduction to 1 Macc. (1:1–9).
7. Hengel, *Judentum*, pp. 332 ff.; Martin Hengel, *Die Zeloten* "Arbeiten zur Geschichte des Spätjudentums und Urchristentums," 1 [Leiden: Brill, 1961]), pp. 308 ff.
8. The prophets Haggai and Zechariah were already hoping for the fall of the Persian empire (ca. 520 B.C.). They thus placed themselves

After the battle of Ipsus (301 B.C.), which marked a temporary conclusion to the struggle among the Diadochi for the heritage of Alexander, Judea, as a part of Palestine, was incorporated into the Ptolemaic Empire. In the following eighty years or so the Jews experienced an age of peace such as was not to be granted them again during the entire four hundred seventy years between Alexander and the Edict of Toleration issued by Antoninus Pius (from 333 B.C. to A.D. 139).[9] This era nevertheless displays a very divided appearance, for in it there took place the first intensive encounter between Palestinian Judaism and the superior Hellenistic civilization. The encounter was not, of course, on the basis of an equal partnership. Palestine—like all the eastern lands ruled by the Ptolemies and Seleucids—had been a "colonial territory." The Diadochi were absolutistic monarchs without legitimation save for the favor of their "fortune," their "*tychē*," in other words the success of their weapons and political acumen. Their power was totally personal, based on fleet and army; the territories they conquered were considered "spear-won land," i.e., the private property of the ruler to be governed as he pleased. Only political prudence and the *philanthrōpia* (friendship toward men) expected of a ruler suggested the desirability of taking into account the needs of the subjects. This system of government achieved its apex of development in the Ptolemaic Empire; this empire was the ruling power in the eastern Mediterranean and was rigorously governed with Greek rationality. Its preeminence was based on a hitherto unknown total mobilization of all economic resources. The wealth gained by systematic "monopolistic"

---

in radical opposition to the expectations of a Deutero-Isaiah; see L. Rost, "Das Problem der Weltmacht in der Prophetie," *ThLZ*, 90 (1965), pp. 248–49.
9. Felix-Marie Abel, *Histoire de la Palestine depuis la conquête d'Alexandre jusqu'à l'invasion arabe* ("Études bibliques" [Paris: Gabalda, 1952]), vol. 1, pp. 22–87; Hengel, *Judentum*, pp. 8–21.

exploitation of agriculture and trade, after the manner of "state capitalism," not only permitted the Ptolemies to maintain the largest fleet and a mighty army of mercenaries, it also enabled them to attract great numbers of young Greeks into the area as officers, technicians, architects, government officials, and physicians. These constituted a new "technocratic" ruling class: the Ptolemaic Empire became the "Greek America," and the methods of government and system of economic and financial exploitation thus introduced continued to dominate Palestine well into the New Testament period.

The Ptolemaic presence in Palestine was primarily military and economic. The important thing was to protect the colonial territory from the old enemy to the north, the Seleucids, and from the marauding Arabs to the east and south. The Ptolemies established a large number of Greek and Macedonian military colonies and promoted the building of fortifications. They garrisoned Jerusalem with foreign troops. Of at least equal importance was the economic exploitation. The taxes collected amounted to several times those collected during the Persian period; little Judea alone (not including the coastal plain, Samaria, and Galilee) yielded up three hundred talents annually, a sum that could not be increased significantly even under Herod and the Romans. The Ptolemaic officials and tax collectors—the detested *telōnēs* or publican now makes his first appearance in the sources—invaded the tiniest village; every plot of ground, every tree, every head of cattle was included. Syria and Palestine became an important supplier of slaves, not only for Egypt, but later also for Greece and Italy. The spread of the Diaspora can be traced in significant measure to the sale of Jewish slaves. Of course the Greeks also brought better methods of agriculture, artificial irrigation, new crops, and an intensification of trade. But all this took place not as "economic assistance" but with the goal of replacing the traditional extensive method of farming with one as intensive as possible, oriented toward production. Large domains in the possession of royal officials, officers, and military colonists became the rule, while the small farmers frequently became tenants. A necessary consequence was the introduction of an hierarchical bureaucracy, the effect of which is depicted tersely and emphatically by Qoheleth (Ecclesiastes):

> If you witness in some province the oppression of the poor,
> And the denial of right and justice,
> Do not be surprised at what goes on,
> For every official has a higher one set over him,
> And the highest keeps watch over them all. (Eccles. 5:7)[10]

In the year 200, Palestine fell like a ripe fruit into the hands of the Seleucid Antiochus III. In his conquest of the land he had the powerful support of the indigenous population, not least the Jews, a sign that the self-assurance of the subject eastern peoples was beginning to take on military overtones. In gratitude for this assistance Antiochus relieved the oppressive burden of taxation in a decree preserved by Josephus.[11] But the cordial relationship with the new ruler did not last too long. In 190 B.C. Antiochus III was beaten decisively by the Romans at Magnesia. For the first time the power of Rome had intervened brutally and directly in the east. The fall of the Hellenistic monarchies was the result.

10. Mikhail Ivanovich Rostovtsev, *Die Hellenistische Welt* (Stuttgart: Kohlhammer, 1955–1956), vol. 1, pp. 196–330, especially pp. 268 ff.; vol. 3, pp. 1131 ff. Avigdor Tcherikover, *Hellenistic Civilization and the Jews* (Philadelphia: Jewish Publication Society, 1959), pp. 1–116; Hengel, *Judentum*, pp. 21–107; cf. the summary in *Verborum veritas, Festschrift Gustav Stählin* (Wuppertal: Brockhaus, 1970), pp. 332 ff.
11. Josephus *Antiquities* xii. 138–44; see Elias Bickermann, *Der Gott der Makkabäer* (Berlin: Schocken, 1937), pp. 50 ff.; Hengel, *Judentum*, pp. 15–16, 53, 493–94.

The reparations in the enormous sum of fifteen thousand talents compelled the Seleucids to increase the financial burden on their subjects once more; they even attempted to lay hands on the sacred Temple treasure.[12] A first such attempt at Jerusalem appears to have failed (2 Maccabees 3); but in 175 B.C. Antiochus IV Epiphanes deposed the legitimate high priest and twice in succession sold the high-priestly office to suitable applicants, who attempted at the same time to carry out a radical reform in Jerusalem, the purpose of which was to transform the Holy City into a Hellenistic polis (city-wide) with the name "Antiocheia" (2 Macc. 4:9). At first this attempt fully to assimilate Judaism to Hellenistic civilization met with a positive response among the Jewish aristocracy in Jerusalem; for example, a gymnasium was built as a special attraction for the fashionable sons of the priests (2 Macc. 4: 12–13). But the clumsiness of the king and the radicalism of the Jewish reformers led to the collapse of this attempt and in 167 B.C. kindled the Maccabean revolt, which ended in 141 B.C., after twenty-six years of seesaw fighting, with the achievement of Jewish independence under the leadership of the Hasmonean dynasty of high priests. The gradual dissolution of the Hellenistic monarchies brought about by Rome strengthened the campaign for independence among the hitherto subject eastern nations.[13]

12. Bengtson, *Griechische Geschichte*, pp. 470 ff.; Tcherikover, *Hellenistic Civilization*, pp. 154 ff.; Hengel, *Judentum*, pp. 17–18, 495–96.
13. Bickermann, *Gott, passim*; Hengel, *Judentum*, pp. 407 ff., 503–55; Tcherikover, *Hellenistic Civilization*, pp. 152–234. On eastern opposition to the Macedonians, see Samuel Kennedy Eddy, *The King Is Dead* (Lincoln: University of Nebraska Press, 1961).

The Jewish Reaction: III

Assimilation and Apocalypticism

What was the reaction within Judaism to Macedonian and Greek imperialism and colonialism after the time of Alexander? Two tendencies can be observed.

On the one hand, people were fascinated by the superior technology and culture of the foreign conquerors, and entered their service as mercenaries or officials. In Palestine the Ptolemaic and Seleucid administration always promoted the hellenization of the indigenous aristocracy and worked closely with it. Thus around the middle of the third century we find a Jewish feudal overlord Tobias in Transjordan acting as commander of a mixed military colony comprising Jews and Greeks; his son Joseph is made Ptolemaic tax collector general for all Palestine and thus to a certain extent the first Jewish banking magnate; two generations later, the latter's grandsons are leading the fight for the radical Hellenistic reform in Jerusalem.[14] In my opinion, Qoheleth also belongs among the feudalistic upper middle class living "with money behind them" (Eccles. 7:12). He was influenced by the contemporary spirit of Hellenistic skepticism and diagnosed the social injustice that was rampant, without however engaging in polemic against it (unlike the later wisdom teacher Ben Sirah [Sirach]).[15]

14. Tcherikover, *Hellenistic Civilization*, pp. 127 ff.; Hengel, *Judentum*, pp. 51 ff., 76 ff., 486 ff.
15. Hengel, *Judentum*, pp. 210–40. Cf. the Erlangen dissertation of R. Braun, 1971.

On the other hand, in the circles of the Hasidim (the devout)[16] renewed attention was paid to the traditions of ancient Israel. In the face of constant demonstrations of Hellenistic military power and of social inequities, new life was breathed into the ancient traditions of the holy war and the social message of the prophets. In contrast to their own impotence and the hopelessness of the present, people placed all their expectations in the prospect of an imminent establishment of God's sovereignty, which must be preceded by the "final battle" of Israel against its oppressors. We find this expectation in the prophecies of Deutero-Zechariah; here Yahweh himself takes the field against the Greeks as warlord, with Judah and Ephraim as his weapons:

> For I have strung Judah my bow,
> I have laid Ephraim the arrow to it;
> I have aroused your sons, O Zion,
> Against the sons of Javan [the Ionians, i.e., the Greeks],
> And made you into the sword of a warrior.[17]   (Zech. 9:13)

Similar tones are heard even from the cautious and fundamentally uneschatological sage Ben Sirah.[18] He lashes out at social injustice in the style of prophetical invective:

> To offer a sacrifice from the possessions of the poor
> Is like killing a son before his father's eyes.
> A crust of bread is life to the destitute,
> And whoever deprives them of it is a murderer.
> To rob your neighbor of his livelihood is to kill him,
> And the man who cheats a worker of his wages sheds blood.
> (Ecclus. 34:20–22)

16. On the earliest history of the "Hasidim" see Otto Plöger, *Theokratie und Eschatologie* ("Wissenschaftliche Monographien zum Alten und Neuen Testament," 2 [Neukirchen: Neukirchner Verlag, 1959]) and Hengel, *Judentum,* pp. 319 ff.
17. See also Zech. 10:3 ff.; 12:6; 14:12 ff.
18. Hengel, *Judentum,* pp. 241–75, 248 ff.

At the same time he prays to God for the eschatological destruction of those who oppress Israel:

> Have pity on us, thou God of all,
> And send thy terror upon all nations.
> Raise thy hand against the heathen [i.e., the Seleucids],
> And let them see thy power.
>
> Rouse thy wrath, pour out thy fury,
> Destroy the adversary, wipe out the enemy.
> Hasten the end and appoint the day.
> Let fiery anger devour the survivors,
> And let the oppressors of thy people meet their doom.
> Crush the head of the prince of Moab,
> Who says, "There is no [god] but me."
>
> (Ecclus. 36: 1–3, 7–10)

This is probably a cryptic reference to the Seleucid rulers, above all Antiochus III, who promoted the royal cult.[19] These militant eschatological voices were significantly strengthened by the attempted Hellenistic reform and the subsequent Maccabean revolt.

The revolt was kindled in 167 B.C. by the establishment of a Seleucid military colony in Jerusalem, in which Jewish apostates joined with pagan military colonists. The radical Hellenistic reformers, in order to break the opposition of the devout, succeeded in obtaining a decree from the king forbidding the practice of the Jewish cult and observance of the Torah; this decree led to the desecration of the Temple. There was a revolt on the part of the simple rural population under the leadership of Mattathias the priest and his five sons,

---

19. On the Ptolemaic and Seleucid ruler-cult, see Fritz Taeger, *Charisma* (Stuttgart: Kohlhammer, 1957–1960), vol. 1, pp. 234 ff.; cf. Elias Bickermann, *Institutions des Séleucides* ("Haut-commissariat de la République française en Syrie et au Liban. Service des antiquités. Bibliothèque archéologique et historique," t. xxvi [Paris: Geuthner, 1938]), pp. 236 ff.; Nilsson, *Geschichte*, vol. 2, pp. 154 ff.; Hengel, *Judentum*, pp. 520 ff.

especially the charismatic Judas Maccabeus; they were joined by the Hasidim, who remained faithful to the law. At first they conducted a guerrilla campaign in the Judean mountains; after three years, however, in 164 B.C. they succeeded in recapturing Jerusalem and the Temple.[20] From this period we have an apocalyptic outline of world history, the so-called Apocalypse of the Symbolic Beasts (Ethiopian Enoch 85—95). It depicts first the oppression of Israel by the nations of the world, especially by the Hellenistic monarchies during the last phase. The crisis is introduced by the revolt of the devout led by Judas Maccabeus. At the moment of greatest distress, when all nations league together to destroy the devout, the great sword of the holy war is given to the latter, that they may put their enemies to flight with it (90:19). Now God finally intervenes directly: all the nations that afflicted and put to death the devout are swallowed up by the earth.[21]

The motif of the holy war appears even more vividly in the Essene War Scroll from Qumran,[22] which goes back in its original form to the period of the Maccabean uprising. Here

20. The most important sources for the Hellenistic reform and the history of events leading up to the Maccabean revolt are the one-sidedly Jewish and Hasmonean account in 1 Maccabees 1—2; the work of Jason of Cyrene, which also draws upon Seleucid sources, summarized in 2 Maccabees 4—6 (see the discussion in Hengel, *Judentum*, pp. 176–83); and Josephus *War* i. 31 ff. and *Antiquities* xii. 237 ff. Remnants of the historical work of Poseidonius, transmitted through Pophyry, are contained in Jerome's commentary on Daniel (MPL 25) in the section on Daniel 11. On the whole topic, see Bickermann, *Gott*, pp. 17 ff.; on Daniel, see note 27.

21. Hengel, *Judentum*, pp. 320–21, 328–29, 342 ff. The text can be found in Emil Kautzsch, ed., *Die Apokryphen und Pseudepigraphen des Alten Testaments* (Tübingen: Mohr, 1900; reprinted Hildesheim: Olms, 1962), vol. 2, pp. 289 ff. Cf. also the Ten Weeks Apocalypse in Eth. En. 91:12 (p. 300).

22. The text can be found in Eduard Lohse, ed., *Die Texte aus Qumran* (München: Kösel, 1964), pp. 180 ff. For a traditio-historical analysis, see Peter von der Osten-Sacken, *Gott und Belial* ("Studien zur Umwelt des Neuen Testaments," 6 [Göttingen: Vandenhoeck & Ruprecht, 1969], pp. 42–72; cf. also Hengel, *Judentum*, p. 32, n. 96.

dualistic apocalypticism is intimately linked with an ideology of revolutionary struggle for freedom. The final eschatological war of the sons of light against the sons of darkness is described. In the original form of the scroll, the sons of darkness include primarily the *kîttîm* of Assyria and "those who blaspheme against the covenant," i.e., the Macedonian Seleucids along with the Jewish apostates (1QM i. 2, 6), or even all the gentile nations (1QM ii. 10 ff.). On the one hand, the account of the war is extremely realistic: it deals with a real war of forty years' duration with a program for "world conquest"; the military details, the equipment and tactical movements of the bodies of troops are all described in loving detail. One might almost think that the author made use of a handbook of Hellenistic military science. On the other hand, the battle is totally utopian and apocalyptic in nature: God himself is the warlord; the angels under the leadership of Michael intervene directly in the battle; the goal is total annihilation of all the sons of darkness. Thus the final battle has to some extent the nature of a judgment over all mankind; at its conclusion there stands the "dominion of Israel over all flesh" (xvii. 7–8). In this fashion the holy war becomes a path to world dominion for the true Israel, identical with the sovereignty of God. It is striking that the devout are also referred to as the "poor" (*'ebyônîm*); in other words, the social motif constitutes an essential part of this apocalyptic battle narrative. The "devout" and the "poor" are one and the same.[23] This tradition of the holy war is then picked up by the various messianic texts of Qumran. The messiah of the line of David is primarily the leader in the eschatological battle; the actual spiritual leader of Israel, on the contrary, is the messianic high priest.[24]

23. Ernst Bammel in *ThW*, vol. 6, pp. 894 ff.
24. On the messianic views held at Qumran, see A. S. van der Woude, *Die messianischen Vorstellungen der Gemeinde von Qumran*

This "militant nationalist" eschatology of the Essenes between their first appearance around 150 B.C. and their destruction by the Romans A.D. 67 stands in strange contrast to the description of them as "pacifists" in Philo and Josephus.[25] Here we must distinguish between their quietistic and ascetic way of life, which so impressed the ancient world, and their highly realistic eschatological expectations. The time of the holy war was near, but not yet present. For a time hatred of the sons of darkness must be restrained. This is made explicit in the Manual of Discipline:

Eternal hatred toward all men of perdition in the spirit of privacy, allowing them their possessions and the works of their hands, like the attitude of the slave toward his master. . . . But everyone is to be zealous for the law and in his day for the day of vengeance. . . .[26]   (1QS ix. 21 ff.)

Thus the spirit of passionate zeal remains fundamental to the Essene movement, which arose amidst the confusion of the Maccabean wars and perished A.D. 67 during the Jewish War. The vast difference between their views and Jesus' command to eschew violence and love one's enemies hardly needs further emphasis.

This justification of hatred and the eager description of the "final battle" as a "day of vengeance" was nevertheless not the only possibility inherent in Jewish apocalypticism. The

("Studia semitca neerlandica" [Assen: Van Gorcum, 1957]; R. Starcky, "Les quatre étapes du messianisme à Qumran," *Revue biblique*, 70 (1963), pp. 480–505.

25. Josephus *War* ii. 135–36; Philo *Quod omnis probus liber sit* 75 ff.; *Hypothetica* 11; cf. Walter Bauer, *Aufsätze und kleine Schriften* (Tübingen: Mohr, 1967), pp. 1–58. According to Bauer, their love of peace was felt by the ancient world to be intimately associated with their community of goods.

26. See Hengel, *Zeloten*, pp. 183–84, and Abraham Schalit, *König Herodes* ("Studia judaica," 4 [Berlin: De Gruyter, 1969]), pp. 719 ff.

Book of Daniel, written in 165 B.C. when the persecutions
were at their height, illustrates a totally different course. It
neither glorifies the struggle for freedom conducted by Judas
Maccabeus nor looks forward to Israel's counterstroke in a
miraculous final battle. In this "time of distress such as has
never been since they became a nation [Israel]" (12:1),
what matters is not armed resistance but only steadfastness
in the face of suffering. "Wise leaders of the nation will give
guidance to the common people; yet for a while they will fall
victims to fire and sword, to captivity and pillage" (11:33).
In other words, the only weapons of the "wise" are words
and teaching. There is only the briefest mention in passing of
the Maccabean uprising, militarily so successful, and that
mention includes criticism: "But these victims will not want
for help, though small, even if many who join them are
insincere" (11:34). In other words, armed revolt ameliorates
the situation of persecution somewhat; but at the same time
it promotes opportunism. Insincere hypocrites always are on
the side of the successful—especially in successful revolutions. The destruction of the godless fourth kingdom is therefore God's autonomous act alone in the eyes of the seer: it
takes place "without the help of hands" (2:44; cf. 9:25).
Thus in Daniel the sovereign reign of God is by no means
prepared for by a battle of national liberation, but only by
the endurance of the suffering community.[27] This sets Daniel
in theologically grounded opposition to the apocalyptic expectation of an eschatological holy war.

27. Cf. Hengel, *Judentum*, pp. 324 ff., and Otto Plöger, *Das Buch
Daniel* ("Kommentar zum Alten Testament," 18 [Gütersloh: Mohn,
1965]), pp. 164–65. J. H. C. Lebram in *VT*, 20 (1970), pp. 507 ff.
totally misjudges the problems and value of the Book of Daniel in
its relationship to the other sources. It is the most "tendentious"
of all.

Jewish Expansion and IV

Internal Opposition

The critical attitude on the part of certain groups of Hasidim toward the prevailing ideology of an eschatological and later nationalistic war of liberation—at this point one might well speak of a "theology of revolution"—surfaced repeatedly during the following, outwardly very successful decades of Jewish history. After the Jews had won total religious freedom in 164/3 B.C., the devout supported a policy of peace with the Seleucids, while Judas wanted to continue the struggle. He fell during the battle against Seleucid hegemony (161 B.C.).[28] The foreign oppressors and their Jewish partisans seemed finally to have won. The guerrilla campaign flared up once more under the leadership of Judas' brothers Jonathan and Simon, but the revolutionary élan had flagged, and Jonathan sought a "realistic compromise." Ten years later (151 B.C.) he achieved success by going over to the side of the Seleucid usurper Alexander Balas, for which he was rewarded with the high-priestly office and the titles "general" and "king's friend" (1 Macc. 10:65). He looked out less for the interests of his new royal overlord than for the extension of Jewish territory at the expense of the Samaritans and the Hellenistic cities. In terms of political realism, the good end justified any means. Jonathan is presumably the "godless

28. 1 Macc. 7:13 ff.; 9:1–19. On the chronology, see Robert Hanhart in Alfred Jepsen and Robert Hanhart, *Untersuchungen zur israelitisch-jüdischen Chronologie* ("Beihefte zur Zeitschrift für die Alttesta-mentliche Wissenschaft," 88 [Berlin: Töpelmann, 1964]), pp. 91 f.

priest" of the Essene *pesharim* (commentaries on the Bible) ; the separation of the "teacher of righteousness" from the Temple cult at Jerusalem was probably a sign of protest on the part of a devout group of Zadokite priests against the religious and political style of the new high priest. The Habakkuk Commentary describes him as follows:

> But when he had come to power in Israel, his heart rebelled, he forsook God and became faithless to the commandments on account of wealth. He plundered and collected wealth from the men of violence, who had rebelled against God. He also took wealth from the gentiles, so that he incurred the sin of wrongdoing.   (1QpHab viii. 9 ff.)

The freedom fighter is here depicted as an avaricious tyrant repaying in their own coin the Jewish apostates who previously had dispossessed the faithful Jews during the period of religious persecution; in other words, he "expropriated the expropriators." Proscription joined with confiscation of property was a proved means of destroying political opponents.[29]

After another ten years (141 B.C.), the Jews achieved political independence under Simon, the brother of Judas and Jonathan. But the "holy war" continued. The struggle for religious freedom turned into a war of national expansion.[30] In an almost uninterrupted series of battles lasting nearly seventy years (143–76 B.C.), Simon, his son John Hyrcanus, and the latter's sons Aristobulus I and Alexander Jannaeus conquered all of Palestine (with the exception of Ashkelon)

29. Hengel, *Judentum*, pp. 407 ff.; see also Gert Jeremias, *Der Lehrer der Gerechtigkeit* ("Studien zur Umwelt des Neuen Testaments," 22 [Göttingen: Vandenhoeck & Ruprecht, 1963]).
30. Emil Schürer, *A History of the Jewish People in the Time of Jesus Christ* (New York: Charles Scribner's Sons, n.d.), div. I, vol. 1, pp. 255–325; Tcherikover, *Hellenistic Civilization*, pp. 235–65; Schalit, *König Herodes*, pp. 196 ff., 529 ff. Cf. H. Kreissig in *Klio*, 43/45 (1945), pp. 174–82.

and great portions of Transjordan. The boundaries of the new Hasmonean state approached those of the Davidic Empire. Thus the reaction to Macedonian imperialism was the nationalistic expansion of the Jewish state, reborn after 446 years of foreign hegemony. The complex interweaving of desire for political power and religious motivation can be illustrated by two points:

(1) In order to preserve the "purity" of the Holy Land and the religious unity of the population, the Hasmoneans compelled the inhabitants of the occupied territories either to submit to compulsory circumcision and become Jews or to emigrate. The Jews' Semitic neighbors such as the Idumeans and Itureans chose circumcision; the inhabitants of the Hellenistic cities often preferred to emigrate.[31]

(2) While imminent eschatological expectations were shared by extensive circles at the beginning of the Maccabean uprising, the Hasmonean rulers now created a present-oriented royal ideology with a religious basis, intended to express the divine election of their dynasty. According to Josephus, John Hyrcanus, the son of Simon, was "accounted worthy by God to occupy the three highest offices: sovereignty over the nation, the honor of the high priesthood, and the gift of prophecy" (Ant. xiii. 299). In other words, this especially successful ruler was accorded almost messianic traits. It was only logical that his sons Aristobulus and Alexander Jannaeus also received the title of king when they received the title of high priest.[32]

On the other hand, the new rulers could not evade their

31. Compulsory circumcision was later required by the Zealots; see Hengel, *Zeloten*, pp. 201 ff. Paul's struggle with the Judaizers in Galatia over the necessity of circumcision for salvation had a long history within Judaism.
32. Cf. Rudolf Meyer in *ThW*, vol. 6, pp. 816, 825; also Test. Levi 5–6; Test. Sim. 5:5, and Test. Reub. 6:12; Schalit, *König Herodes*, pp. 743–44.

political destiny, that is, the influence of the superior Hellenistic civilization against which their fathers had rebelled. The system of government and taxation returned increasingly to the tried and true Hellenistic practices. Alexander Jannaeus issued coins bearing Greek inscriptions and—since the Jewish militia was exhausted by the continual wars—hired gentile mercenaries from Asia Minor. Furthermore, the life style of the rulers and the new military aristocracy hardly differed from that of the other hellenized eastern monarchies.[33]

This stark contrast between ideological claims and politico-social and ethical reality led to a new schism within Palestinian Judaism. Party conflict flared up once more in all its bitterness. The Hasidic opposition took shape in the Pharisees, a new party with strong lay influence, while the Hasmoneans drew their support from the Sadducees, the priestly and military aristocracy.[34] Under Alexander Jannaeus violent rebellion actually broke out, which he suppressed cruelly: he had eight hundred Pharisees crucified in Jerusalem while he feasted with his concubines; eight thousand fled into exile.[35] After his death (76 B.C.), his widow sided with the Pharisees,

33. Schalit, *König Herodes*, pp. 106, 167–68, 196–206, 530–31; cf. Hengel, *Judentum*, pp. 11–12, 119–20, 412–13. An example of the way of life of the new military aristocracy is furnished by the tomb of the Jewish pirate captain Jason in Jerusalem: L. Y. Rahmani *et al.* in *'Atiqot*, 4 (1964), pp. 1–40; cf. Pierre Benoit in *Israel Exploration Journal*, 17 (1967), pp. 112–13.

34. See the excellent articles on the Pharisees and Sadducees by R. Meyer in *ThW*, vol. 9, pp. 12 ff., 23 ff. and vol. 7, pp. 35 ff.

35. Josephus *Antiquities* xiii. 380, supplemented by 4QpNah i. 7 (Lohse, *Texte*, p. 262). The Persian punishment of crucifixion was introduced into Judea in the Hellenistic period. According to Q. C. Rufus iv. 4. 17, Alexander had two thousand inhabitants of Tyre crucified on the coast. Other examples are cited by K. Latte in August Friedrich von Pauly, *Realencyclopädie der classischen Altertumswissenschaft* (Stuttgart: Metzler, 1903–   ), supp. vol. 7, pp. 1606–1607; and Martin Hengel, *Nachfolge und Charisma* ("Beihefte zur Zeit-

who now in turn took bloody vengeance on the Sadducees. Thus the religious and social renewal of the Jewish nation, inaugurated by the Maccabean revolt, foundered on the lust for power of the new dynasty that came to the throne through the "revolution," and ended in a new political and religious catastrophe.[36]

---

schrift für die Neutestamentliche Wissenschaft," 34 [Berlin: Töpelmann, 1968]), p. 64, nn. 76 and 77. On its use in the Roman period, see below, note 96.
36. Schalit, *König Herodes*, pp. 539 ff.

Roman Rule   V

and Herod

In the meantime the political situation in the eastern Mediterranean had changed completely. Rome had entered upon the inheritance of the old Hellenistic monarchies. As late as the second century B.C. a desired ally of the Jews in their struggle for freedom against the Seleucids (1 Maccabees 8), it now appeared in the east as protector of Hellenistic civilization—and that means the Hellenistic cities—in the face of threats on the part of the "barbarians," among whom aggressive Judea could be counted. In 63 B.C. the struggle for power between the two sons of Alexander Jannaeus, Hyrcanus II and Aristobulus II, gave Pompey the excuse he needed to intervene. After three months of siege he stormed the hill of the Temple, bitterly defended by supporters of Aristobulus, and entered the Holy of Holies. The Jewish state was shattered and the freedom of the Greek cities in Palestine restored.[37] Both the Essene Habakkuk Commentary and the Pharisaic Psalms of Solomon recount in one breath the ruin of the humbled Hasmonean dynasty and the cruelty and hubris of Roman imperialism. The catastrophe was interpreted as a just punishment for the sins of the people and

37. Schürer, *History*, div. 1, vol. 1, pp. 313 ff.; Schalit, *König Herodes*, pp. 1–36; Hermann Bengtson, *Grundriss der römischen Geschichte* ("Handbuch der Altertumswissenschaft," 3. Abt., 5. Teil [München: Beck, 1967–   ]), vol. 1, pp. 203–204, 243–44. On the struggle against Roman expansion, see Harald Fuchs, *Der geistige Widerstand gegen Rom* (2nd ed.; Berlin: De Gruyter, 1964); J. Denninger, *Der politische Widerstand gegen Rom in Griechenland* (1971).

their rulers; but at the same time men prayed ardently that God would avenge the blasphemy committed by the foreigners and that the messiah of the Davidic line would come soon.[38]

Judea was once more a province subject to arbitrary foreign control; the dream of a Jewish empire was shattered. The Jews now felt the full harshness of the Roman financial system, administered by the infamous associations of tax collectors.[39] The situation was aggravated by repeated attempts at rebellion on the part of Aristobulus and his sons, as well as by the Roman Civil War, in which the party in power at any given moment plundered the subject provinces with particular brutality. The population of entire cities was frequently sold into slavery,[40] sometimes because they rebelled, sometimes because they could not raise the military levies. Caesar, it is true, granted the Jews once more a measure of independence (47 B.C.), according the high priest Hyrcanus II the title "ethnarch"; but the real power resided in his advisers, the only superficially judaized Idumean Antip-

38. The text of the Habakkuk Commentary will be found in Lohse, *Texte,* pp. 228 ff.; the text of the Psalms of Solomon is in A. Rahlfs, ed., *Septuaginta,* vol. 2, pp. 471 ff.; a translation by R. Kittel will be found in Kautzsch, *Apokryphen,* vol. 2, pp. 130 ff. See especially Ps. Sol. 1; 2; 8; 17:4–20.

39. Schalit, *König Herodes,* pp. 279–80, 294 ff.; cf. pp. 72–73, 296 ff.; Otto Michel in *ThW,* vol. 8, pp. 95 ff.

40. In Tarichea, for example, thirty thousand Jews were sold into slavery after a revolt (Josephus *Antiquities* xiv. 120; = *War* i. 180); the same happened in 43 B.C. to the inhabitants of the toparchy capitals of Gophna, Emmaus, and Lydda (*Antiquities* xiv. 272, 275; = *War* i. 219–20; Schalit, *König Herodes,* pp. 47–48). Cf. Hans Volkmann, *Massenversklavungen der Einwohner eroberter Städte in der hellenistisch-römischen Zeit* ("Akademie der Wissenschaften und der Literatur, Mainz. Abhandlungen der Geistes- und Sozialwissenschaftlichen Klasse," 1961:3 [Wiesbaden: Steiner, 1961]), pp. 181 ff. Such mass enslavement was a favorite means of Roman political violence; see below, p. 29.

ater and his sons Phasael and Herod.[41] The great Parthian invasion in 40 B.C. seemed to give the Hasmonean Antigonus, the son of the murdered Aristobulus II, a final chance to recapture the throne of his fathers and put an end to foreign domination. But shortly afterward the senate named Herod, a "half Jew" who had fled to Rome, "king of the Jews." Only after three years of seesaw warfare against bitter Jewish opposition was he able, with Roman assistance, to capture Jerusalem (37 B.C.). Antigonus—the last Jewish king of the Hasmonean dynasty—fell victim at Antioch to the ax of the Roman executioner.[42]

The thirty-three-year reign of Herod (37–4 B.C.) presents a very divided picture.[43] Even the sources used by Josephus exhibit sharply divided judgments.[44] The multitude of magnificent structures whose remains are still visible today point to a glorious reign, the likes of which was not seen in Judea before or since. In addition, the fact that outwardly peace reigned during his regime and the perpetual revolts and wars came to an end could be evaluated positively. This circum-

41. Josephus *Antiquities* xiv. 127–216; cf. Schalit, *König Herodes*, pp. 36 ff., 777 ff.
42. Josephus *Antiquities* xiv. 330–491; cf. Schalit, *König Herodes*, pp. 74–97; Karl-Heinz Ziegler, *Die Beziehungen zwischen Rom und dem Partherreich* (Wiesbaden: Steiner, 1964).
43. We possess the frankly anti-Jewish presentation by Hugo Willrich, *Das Haus des Herodes* ("Bibliothek der klassischen Altertumswissenschaft," 6 [Heidelberg: Winter, 1929]), and the frankly anti-Herodian and anti-Roman presentation of Joseph Klausner in his *Bi-yeme bayit sheni* (4th ed.; Jerusalem: Mada, 1954) vol. 4. By way of contrast, Walter Otto, *Herodes* (Stuttgart: Metzler, 1913; = Paulys *Realencyclopädie*, supp. vol. 2, pp. 2–200), attempts to present an account *sine ira et studio*. In similar fashion, Schalit (*König Herodes*) takes pains to give a fair presentation; cf. also Hengel, *Zeloten*, pp. 324–31, where I have attempted to depict the reign of Herod with a view to its consequences for the development of the Jewish liberation movement.
44. On the conflict in the sources used by Josephus, see Hengel, *Zeloten*, p. 13, n. 5, and p. 324, n. 2. In his *Antiquities*, Josephus used the historical work of Nicholas of Damascus, a friend of Herod; but he also drew on a fiercely anti-Herodian source of unknown origin.

stance was of course less to his credit than it was the fruit of
the *Pax Romana* provided by Augustus, the peace enjoyed by
the whole Roman Empire. Herod in fact took Augustus as his
model, and considered it his primary task, at whatever cost,
to integrate notoriously turbulent Judea into this *Pax
Romana.*[45] The Jews, to be sure, had to pay a high price for
this "law and order": a merciless despotism and an un-
exampled harshness toward all enemies, real and supposed.
The only thing that counted for Herod was power; to power
he would unhesitatingly sacrifice all other considerations. An
army of foreign mercenaries far exceeding the needs of the
country, numerous strongholds and military colonies, as well
as an army of informers held the unwilling Jewish population
in check and created an atmosphere of permanent fear.[46] In
line with Hellenistic political principles the king promoted
trade and agriculture, and set up a strict and efficient administration; but in the last analysis everything was devoted to the
optimal exploitation of the land. Since the annual income of
1000–2000 talents in taxes was insufficient to meet his lavish
expenditures, he unlocked additional sources of income
through forced "donations" and through confiscation of the
property of the multitude who fell victim to his arbitrary
justice. In this way he turned a great portion of the land into
his personal property, distributing parts of it in turn to his
favorites.[47] After Judea was transformed into a Roman

45. Schalit, *König Herodes*, pp. 412 ff., 554 ff.
46. Political denunciation promoted and encouraged by the state is a
typical invention of the Hellenistic monarchies, adopted by Herod.
For an early example, see the Ptolemaic decree on the declaration of
slaves and cattle in Palestine in Friedrich Preisigke, *Sammelbuch
griechischer Urkunden aus Ägypten* (Strassburg: Trübner, 1915), no.
8008; Eccles. 10:20; also 2 Macc. 3:7; 4:1; 6:11. With reference to
Herod, see Josephus *Antiquities* xv. 285 ff., 366 ff.; = *War* i. 570, 573;
Schalit, *König Herodes*, pp. 315 ff.; Hengel, *Zeloten,* p. 326. Even
rabbinic tradition (Baba Batra 4a) confirms this situation.
47. Schalit (*König Herodes,* pp. 256 ff.) judges Herod's "financial
policies" too positively; cf. Hengel, *Zeloten*, p. 329.

province, this "royal land" was auctioned off for the benefit of the Roman fisc. The structure of large estates worked by tenants, depicted in Jesus' parables as the prevailing system in Palestine, here has its beginnings.[48] After Herod's death, the Jewish population complained bitterly about the unbearable burden of the taxes he had imposed.[49]

While Herod mercilessly extirpated the pro-Hasmonean aristocracy of the Sadducees, the Pharisees were at first not fundamentally hostile toward the king. During the siege of Jerusalem, the two leading Pharisees Sameas and Pollio (Shammai and Hillel?) are reputed to have advised surrendering the city on the basis of the argument that the sins of the people made it impossible for them to escape.[50] Of course Herod's contempt for the Torah made the enmity of the most influential Jewish party a foregone conclusion sooner or later: twice the Pharisees refused the loyalty oath the king had imposed on the people;[51] their anti-Herodian messianic propaganda even gained entrance in the palace and among the family of Herod.[52] Pharisaic criticism was not least directed against his Idumean origin, referring to Deut. 17:15: "You must not appoint a foreigner over you."[53] Shortly

48. For a discussion of demesne economy and tenant farming in Palestine in connection with the parables of Jesus, see M. Hengel, "Das Gleichnis von den Weingärtnern Mc 12, 1–12 im Lichte der Zenonpapyri und der rabbinischen Gleichnisse," *ZNW*, 59 (1968), pp. 9–31. Here, too, the groundwork for the system was laid in the early Hellenistic period under the Ptolemies (Hengel, *Judentum*, pp. 33–34, 67 ff.).

49. Josephus *Antiquities* xvii. 204, 310; = *War* ii. 4, 86.

50. Josephus *Antiquities* xiv. 176; cf. xv. 3; see Schalit, *König Herodes*, pp. 98 ff., 768 ff.

51. Josephus *Antiquities* xv. 368–71; xvii. 41 ff.; see Schalit, *König Herodes*, pp. 316 ff.

52. Josephus *Antiquities* xvii. 43 ff.; see Schalit, *König Herodes*, pp. 630–31. This account is important evidence of apocalyptic tendencies among the Pharisees at the time of Herod.

53. This passage plays a central role in the rabbinic account of Herod (Baba Batra 3b/4a); cf. Schalit, *König Herodes*, pp. 692–93, and Hengel, *Zeloten*, pp. 323–24.

before his death, radical Pharisees and their students destroyed the image of an eagle added to the Temple by Herod, who ordered the "felons" burned alive. The devout were also enraged that, contrary to the law, Herod sold Jewish "thieves" and "criminals"—undoubtedly including members of the opposition—as slaves for foreign countries, for example, to work in the state mines.[54] Herod attempted to create his own "royal ideology" as a kind of Jewish variant on the cult of the emperor, which he vigorously promoted in the non-Jewish parts of the land.[55] This included an attempt to demonstrate his pure Jewish descent—according to Schalit, even Davidic descent.[56] The king also appealed to his unique political successes and his glorious project of rebuilding the Temple. His rise to power and great success in all he attempted, he claimed, was a gift of God, proving that God had elected him king; the rebuilding of the Temple was intended to express his royal gratitude toward God. The peace and happiness of the nation were guaranteed not by utopian expectation of a future messianic kingdom, but by the present rule of the king together with the *Pax Romana*.[57] The group of Herodians, who also appear in the Gospels, were presumably

54. Josephus *Antiquities* xvii. 149–63; = *War* i. 648–55; Hengel, *Zeloten*, pp. 107–108, 221, 264–65.
55. Schalit, *König Herodes*, pp. 460–82. On Herod's demand that the emperor cult be practiced in non-Jewish territory, see Hengel, *Zeloten*, pp. 105 ff. For a general discussion of the emperor cult, see Taeger, *Charisma*, vol. 2.
56. Abraham Schalit, "Die frühchristliche Überlieferung über die Herkunft der Familie des Herodes," *Annual of the Swedish Theological Institute*, 2 (1963), pp. 109–60; *idem*, *König Herodes*, pp. 473–74.
57. Josephus *Antiquities* xv. 383: "I believe that, in accordance with God's will, I have led the Jewish nation to such good fortune as it never enjoyed before"; cf. xv. 387 and the discussion in Schalit, *König Herodes*, pp. 470 ff. Cf. also Matt. 2:1 ff.

supporters of his dynasty and thus at the same time representatives of such an Herodian royal ideology.[58]

58. Mark 3:6; 12:13; Matt. 22:16. See Elias Bickermann, "Les Héro-
diens," *Revue biblique*, 47 (1938), pp. 184 ff.; Schalit, *König Herodes*,
pp. 479 ff.

The Eschatological   VI

Liberation Movement

The unreality of these claims is revealed by the rebellions
that broke out with pent-up fury immediately after Herod's
death.[59] The whole land was filled with bloody disorders.
While these were being put down at Jerusalem by the Roman
governor of Syria, Quintilius Varus (who had two thousand
"agitators" crucified round about Jerusalem as a deterrent[60]),
in the Jordan valley a band of guerrillas gathered around a
slave of Herod named Simon and destroyed the Herodian
palaces; in Judea a former shepherd named Athronges and
his four brothers fought with amazing success, and were able
to hold out for years against the troops of Herod's son
Archelaus. In Galilee, Judas (presumably the later founder
of the Zealot movement) plundered the arsenal of Herod at
Sepphoris, three miles north of Nazareth, the home of Jesus;
the inhabitants of the ill-fated town were sold into slavery by
Varus as punishment. All three agitators had one thing in
common: they claimed royal office, which probably means
that they appeared as messianic pretenders.[61] This character-

59. Hengel, *Zeloten*, pp. 331–36.
60. Josephus *Antiquities* xvii. 293 ff.; = *War* ii. 73 ff.; cf. Assumption
of Moses 6:8–9; Hengel, *Zeloten*, p. 333, n. 5.
61. Hengel, *Zeloten*, pp. 297 ff. The criticism of M. de Jonge in
Novum testamentum, 8 (1966), pp. 145–46, passes over the fact that
except in *Antiquities* xx. 200 Josephus never uses the term *"christos"*
for Jesus, and in that one passage uses it only as a proper name. For
political reasons Josephus suppresses almost all notice of Jewish
messianic hopes; only in the context of Dan. 7:13 ff. and Num. 24:17

29

istic suggests that messianic expectations had grown particularly intense during the reign of Herod, and that Jewish Palestine had become a politico-religious tinderbox.

New unrest broke out in A.D. 6 when Augustus, acting upon a complaint of the Samaritans, deposed Archelaus for mismanagement and turned Judea into a Roman province under an equestrian prefect.[62] As a consequence, a census had to be conducted in Judea for the assessment of head and land taxes; the Jewish population in part understood this obvious directive as meaning that the Holy Land was being made the private property of the emperor and its population enslaved. On the basis of this notion the founders of the Zealot movement, Judas the Galilean and Zadok the Pharisee, forged a highly effective religious ideology of eschatological struggle for liberation. This ideology could be considered the final consequence of long bitter experience with gentile hegemony. Its basic axioms were ardent expectation of God's reign and fanatical zeal for the law. The following propositions were involved:[63]

does he give a cautious hint of them (see Hengel, *Zeloten*, p. 245). What is crucial is rather his use of the term *"basileus"* (king), which has messianic significance in this revolutionary and apocalyptic context. This holds true also for the inscription on Jesus' cross (Mark 15: 26 parr.), and for the later pseudomessiah Andreas Lukuas during the revolt in Cyrenaica and Egypt (A.D. 115–117). See Avigdor Tcherikover, *Corpus papyrorum judaicorum* (Cambridge, Mass.: Harvard University Press, 1957–1964), vol. 1, pp. 88 ff.: "Each of these 'kings' was regarded by himself, as well by his followers, as the 'Messiah,' sent by God to humiliate the heathen world and to rescue the Jews from their bondage to Rome" (p. 90). Similar considerations apply also to Bar Kochba.

62. Josephus *Antiquities* xvii. 342 ff., 355; xviii. 2; = *War* ii. 111, 117; cf. Dio Cassius lv. 27. 6; Schürer, *History*, div. I, vol. 2, pp. 41 ff.; Hengel, *Zeloten*, pp. 336 ff. The title "procurator" was not commonly used until the time of Claudius. On his competency see Adrian Nicholas Sherwin-White, *Roman Society and Roman Law in the New Testament* (Oxford: Clarendon, 1963), pp. 1–24.

63. Hengel, *Zeloten*, pp. 78–93; idem, *Was Jesus a Revolutionist?* (Facet Books—Biblical Series [Philadelphia: Fortress Press, 1971]), pp. 11 ff., pp. 11–13, n. 39; "War Jesus Revolutionär? Sechs Thesen

Expectation of God's kingship and lordship made it appear blasphemous to refer to the emperor as "king" and "lord." Since the emperor demanded to be worshiped as god throughout the entire Hellenistic east, this requirement could be understood as an extension of the first commandment: You shall have no other gods besides me. In a sense, what was at stake here was a theocentrically grounded desire to be free of all rulers.[64]

As a consequence, payment of taxes to the emperor appeared perforce to be idolatry and apostasy from God, ending in self-imposed slavery.[65] But God had called Israel to freedom. In addition, the census involved in the tax program violated Old Testament tradition (2 Samuel 24).

The coming of God's reign depended on human "revolutionary activity," and could not simply be awaited quietisticly and passively. It was realized only in active cooperation with God. The rabbinate was later to condemn the Zealot movement for wanting "to hasten the end."[66]

This cooperation between God and the "true Israel" took

---

eines Neutestamentlers," *EvKomm*, 12 (1969), pp. 694–96; Oscar Cullmann, *Jesus und die Revolutionären seiner Zeit* (2nd ed.; Tübingen: Mohr, 1970), pp. 13 ff.

64. Hengel, *Zeloten*, pp. 93–114.

65. *Ibid.*, pp. 132–45; cf. Schalit, *König Herodes*, pp. 267–98. Tertullian calls the Roman land and head tax, levied on the basis of the census, *"notae captivitatis"* (*Apolog.* xiii, 6).

66. Hengel, *Zeloten*, pp. 127 ff.; cf. *idem, Was Jesus a Revolutionist?* p. 20, n. 60. According to Josephus, "synergistic" cooperation with God typified Pharisaic theology in contrast to Essene determinism and Sadducaic emphasis on complete freedom of the will; see his *War* ii. 163; *Antiquities* vi. 20; xiii. 172; xviii. 13. It is certainly no accident when Dorothee Sölle (*EvKomm* 4 [1971], p. 20) demands for the new "political theology" an "understanding of man as *cooperator dei*, not as recipient of commands or grace," and defines this as "a new understanding of repentance as a real transformation and conversion." For the Zealots, "conversion" consisted in accepting solidarity with the revolutionary action, a step that demanded unconditional readiness for self-sacrifice, indeed for martyrdom; cf. Hengel, *Zeloten*, pp. 265 ff. Today theology is once more faced with the danger of an acute "Zealot Judaism."

place in the form of a "holy war,"[67] which had to be conducted by means of guerrilla warfare, a situation like the
beginnings of the Maccabean rebellion before the outbreak of
the Jewish War. The zealots had their bases in the numerous
caves in the desert of Judah, whence they launched attacks
upon the settled regions where they found support among the
oppressed rural population. The guerrillas retreated once
more into the desert after their surprise attacks, frequently
leaving the Jewish peasants to bear the vengeance of the
Roman occupation troops. Driven from their villages, they
would recruit the bands in the desert.[68] Individual groups
later advanced as far as Jerusalem, where they executed
summary justice and kidnapped high-placed personalities in
order to extort the release of prisoners.[69] The ultimate goal
was to stir up a general popular rebellion against Rome, which
was seen as the prerequisite for God's intervention.[70] The
Romans and their Jewish partisans, for their part, considered
the freedom fighters not regular "enemies" (*hostes*) but ban-

67. Hengel, *Zeloten*, pp. 165 ff., 265–96. On this point they could cite
Old Testament apocalyptic traditions as well as revolutionary "practice" since the victorious Maccabean revolt; see above, pp. 000 and
Hengel, *Judentum*, pp. 31–32, 273 ff., 343–44, 530 ff.
68. Hengel, *Zeloten*, pp. 42 ff., 255 ff., 334–35, 348–61; cf. *idem, Was
Jesus a Revolutionist?* p. 13.
69. Josephus recounts a whole series of daring exploits that exhibit
great similarity to present-day guerrilla tactics. Around A.D. 50, for
example, they ambushed an "imperial slave"—probably an official of
the *fiscus Caesaris* conveying funds—on the highway between Jerusalem and Caesarea. As punishment, the procurator had the sur-
rounding villages pillaged and their elders brought forth in chains,
probably because they had supported the brigands: Josephus *Antiquities* xx. 113–14; = *War* ii. 228–29; Hengel, *Zeloten*, p. 353; cf. pp.
355 ff. Later, a few years before the outbreak of the Jewish War, they
kidnapped the secretary of Eleazar, the captain of the Temple and son
of the high priest, and exchanged him for ten *sicarii* arrested by the
procurator Albinus; Josephus *Antiquities* xx. 208 ff.; Hengel, *Zeloten*,
pp. 360–61.
70. Hengel, *Zeloten*, pp. 288 ff., 361 ff.

dits and brigands (*latrones*, Greek *lēstai*) or assassins (*sicarii*).[71]

God's sovereignty was conceived in earthly, totally realistic terms; it was identical with the sovereignty of the people of God and associated with the ideal of political liberty. The term "liberty" or "freedom" (*hērût*) appears for the first time on the coins issued during the Jewish revolt A.D. 66–67; the exodus from Egypt was also interpreted as the realization of *hērût*, providing a model for all time.[72] An additional fundamental component was social justice.[73] This included the abolition of debtor subjection—when the Zealots conquered Jerusalem A.D. 66, the first thing they did was to destroy the city archives with its loan documents—the breaking up of large estates, and the liberation of the slaves.[74] Thus the Zealot movement was not least a movement of social revolution based on religious principles.

71. *Ibid.*, pp. 24–54.
72. *Ibid.*, pp. 114–27; cf. also Cecil Roth, "The Historical Implications of the Jewish Coinage of the First Revolt," *Israel Exploration Journal*, 12 (1962), pp. 33–46.
73. Hengel, *Zeloten*, pp. 136 ff., 341–42, 358–59, 362–63; cf. *idem*, *Was Jesus a Revolutionist?* p. 14, nn. 47 and 48; *ZNW*, 59 (1968), pp. 19 ff.; Günther Baumbach, "Das Freiheitsverständnis in der zelotischen Bewegung," in *Das ferne und das nahe Wort (Festschrift L. Rost)* ("Beihefte zur Zeitschrift für die Alttestamentliche Wissenschaft," 105 [Berlin: Töpelmann, 1967]), pp. 11–18. Even in the Egyptian Diaspora the lower strata of the Jewish population were open to Zealot ideas; see A. Tcherikover, *Corpus*, vol. 1, pp. 67–68. The dissertation of H. Kreissig, *Die sozialen Zusammenhänge des jüdischen Krieges* (Berlin, Humboldt-Universität, 1965) contains a wealth of valuable material on the social history of the period, but draws conclusions that are too extreme on account of its perspective of dogmatic Leninism. It considers the Jewish liberation movement exclusively as a "class struggle" and seeks to eliminate the crucial religious element almost totally.
74. Josephus *War* ii. 427; see Hengel, *Zeloten*, pp. 368–69. On the freeing of the slaves by Simon bar Giora, see Josephus *War* iv. 508 and Otto Michel in *NTS*, 14 (1967/68), pp. 402–403. Throughout the entire history of the ancient world the remission of debts and freeing of slaves were among the basic demands of social reform; see Bengtson, *Griechische Geschichte*, pp. 402 (King Agis IV of Sparta),

Although we do not possess much data about the details of the struggle for freedom, we do know that Judas gained many adherents, and only the influence of the high priest prevented a general uprising. The Zealot movement was forced to retreat into the desert, where, however, it was able to keep itself alive until the outbreak of the Jewish War.[75] Two sons of Judas Galileus were crucified toward the end of the forties by the procurator Julius Alexander, a Jewish renegade and nephew of Philo of Alexandria. A son or grandson of Judas, Menahem, gave the signal for the revolt with the capture of the fortress of Masada in the year A.D. 66; at the same time, the priests in Jerusalem, who had been won over to the cause of the revolution, ceased offering sacrifices in the Temple on behalf of the emperor, thus breaking officially with Rome. Menahem took over leadership of the revolt in the capital, and under his leadership the Jews succeeded in capturing the

---

491 (the Achaean League before its last war with Rome, 146 B.C.), 492 (the usurper Aristonikos in Pergamon with his utopian "sun state"), 497 (Mithridates VI of Pontus). In the last three instances the measures were directed against Rome. For an interpretive discussion, see Joseph Vogt, *Sklaverei und Humanität* ("Historia-Einzelschriften," 8 [Wiesbaden: Steiner, 1965]), pp. 20–68. For Judaism the freeing of slaves and remission of debts were determined by the regulations governing the year of release: Lev. 25; Deut. 15:1 ff.; 31:10–11; cf. also Exod. 21:1–2; Jer. 34:8 ff. In the Qumran fragment 11QMelch, with reference to Isa. 61:1–2, the onset of the eschaton is interpreted as the onset of the "year of liberation"; see A. S. van der Woude in *Oudtestamentische Studien*, 14 (1965), pp. 354–73. Among the Zealots, too, these requirements probably had an eschatological background. On the other hand, it is a striking fact that Hillel, the leader of the liberal Pharisaic wing, gave a special ruling that made it possible to render the year of release a dead letter; see George Foot Moore, *Judaism in the First Centuries of the Christian Era* (Cambridge, Mass.: Harvard University Press, 1927–1930), vol. 3, p. 80, n. 25; D. Correns, ed., "Schebiit," in *Die Mischna*, ed. by G. Beer (Giessen: Töpelmann, 1912–   ), 1.5 (1960), 16, 155–56 on 10.3.

75. Hengel, *Zeloten*, pp. 336 ff. The speech of Gamaliel in Acts 5:37 may presuppose that Judas was killed in the course of his attempted revolt. The movement nevertheless survived.

palace of Herod. A short time afterward, however, he was treacherously murdered by rival priests during a visit to the Temple, presumably on account of his messianic claims.[76]

Here we see revealed the point at which the Jewish freedom fighters failed long before Rome intervened with all its power. As soon as they had reached their goal and driven the whole nation into war with Rome, the revolutionary "united front" disintegrated. In fact, five different revolutionary factions tore each other to shreds under their ambitious leaders, with first one group and then another on top, in a bloody fight for the correct ideology and possession of power that lasted until the army of Titus stood before the gates of Jerusalem.[77] This disintegration of the Jewish liberation movement at the critical moment may be connected with a strong anarchistic tendency that would not allow a single leader actually to seize power.

The movement emanating from Judas the Galilean was only one of the various Jewish "factions," of which Josephus describes four. He does not mention the actual name of the faction established by Judas, presumably for defamatory reasons; in one passage he calls it the "fourth philosophical sect," which suggests a well-defined ideological platform, while elsewhere he speaks of the "*sicarii*," a term based on their tactic of assassination. They probably had in mind the Old Testament example of Phinehas, who slew a Jewish lawbreaker *in flagranti* (Num. 25:1–15), when they called themselves *qannā'îm*, i.e., "zealots" (Greek *zēlotai*). It is true that Josephus, with one exception (*Bellum* ii. 444), reserves this honorable religious term for a small priestly splinter

76. On the dynasty of Judas of Galilee, see Hengel, *Zeloten*, p. 338. Cf. Josephus *Antiquities* xx. 102; *War* ii. 433–48; and the discussion in Hengel, *Zeloten*, pp. 352–53, 365 ff.
77. Hengel, *Zeloten*, pp. 376 ff.; Schürer, *History*, div. I, vol. 2, pp. 235 ff.; cf. Hengel, *Was Jesus a Revolutionist?* pp. 13–14.

group during the Jewish War; but his outspoken pro-Roman and anti-Zealot bias renders his data on this point not absolutely trustworthy.[78]

The adherents of the struggle against Rome exercised their greatest influence among the younger generation and the impoverished rural population. The inhabitants of the border provinces of Galilee, Idumea, and Perea also appeared more favorable to the rebellion, while the urban population of Jerusalem, which set the fashion, as well as the two major Galilean towns Tiberias and Sepphoris rejected revolutionary adventures for the most part and were ready to listen to the aristocratic high priests and Sadducees.[79] The moderate Pharisees of the school of Hillel, under the leadership of Gamaliel, the son or grandson of Hillel and teacher of Paul (Acts 22:3; cf. 5:34), also supported this attitude. Little was altered by the fact that between A.D. 6 and 41 the clan of Annas held the office of high priest most of the time: first Annas himself (A.D. 6–14), later his son-in-law Caiaphas, whose tenure was especially long (A.D. 18–37). According to Josephus (*Ant.* xx. 198), all five of his sons succeeded to the high-priestly office. They made good use of their eminent position to line their own purses through the flourishing sacrificial traffic, and purchased themselves a good relationship with the Roman prefects by means of massive bribes. The prefects in turn had to rely on the high-priestly aristocracy to mediate be-

---

78. Hengel, *Zeloten*, pp. 61 ff., 160 ff. On the question of terminology, see also the discussion of G. Baumbach's theses in Hengel, *Was Jesus a Revolutionist?* pp. 11–13, n. 39. The movement could be termed an "underground organization"; see Hengel, *Zeloten*, p. 88. Its characterization as the "left wing" of the Pharisees has recently been disputed, without cogent reasons, by G. Baumbach and others. Josephus —himself a Pharisee—is forced to admit that the movement's cofounder Zadok was a Pharisee (*Antiquities* xviii. 4 ff.); cf. Hengel, *Zeloten*, pp. 89 ff.; *idem., Was Jesus a Revolutionist?* pp. 11–13, n. 39 (for the literature); and R. Meyer in *ThW*, vol. 9, pp. 27–28.
79. Hengel, *Zeloten*, pp. 333–34, 335, 342, n. 5.

tween them and the difficult Jewish people.[80] Even the excesses and brutality of a Pilate, depicted in detail by Josephus, did not lead to open rebellion, although he frequently made it his object to humiliate the Jews and offend their religious sensibilities.[81] The description of Pilate recorded a few years after his removal from office, written by one of his contemporaries, Philo of Alexandria, speaks for itself: "He was of a hard disposition, brutal and pitiless." His administration was in the same vein: "Corruption, violence, robbery, brutality, extortion, and execution without trial" were the order of the day (*Leg. ad C.* 299–305). A vivid illustration occurs in Luke 13:1, in which Jesus is told about "the Galileans whose blood Pilate had mixed with their sacrifices." Obviously the Roman prefect had ordered the execution of a number of Galileans during the Passover festival when they came intending to slaughter their Passover lambs in the Temple.

The attempt of the insane Caligula, on the other hand, to compel the Jews to set up a statue of him in the Temple at Jerusalem led the land to the brink of public catastrophe: the Jews threatened to take up arms should the emperor persist in enforcing this blasphemy, the spring plowing was left undone, brigandage increased. Only the assassination of the emperor prevented open rebellion (A.D. 41).[82] Claudius appointed the flexible and nationalistic Herod Agrippa I as king of all Judea. This eased the tense situation, but the king's premature death after three years on the throne (A.D. 41–44) and the transfor-

---

80. Cf. Joseph Blinzler, *Der Prozess Jesus* (4th ed.; Regensburg: Pustet, 1969), pp. 129 ff.
81. Josephus *Antiquities* xviii. 55–62; = *War* ii. 169–77. Cf. Blinzler, *Prozess*, pp. 260 ff.; Hengel, *Zeloten*, pp. 213, 222, 344 ff.
82. Josephus *Antiquities* xviii. 261–309; = *War* ii. 184–203; cf. Philo *Legatio ad Gaium* beginning with §197, with the comments of E. M. Smallwood in *Philonis Alexandrii Legatio ad Gaium* (Leiden: Brill, 1961) and Hengel, *Zeloten*, pp. 109 ff., 348.

mation of Judea into a Roman province once more laid the groundwork for renewed conflict. The situation was made worse by the great famine of the mid-forties, the increasingly corrupt administration of the procurators after Felix, and the concomitant sense of insecurity and misery.[83] The repressive violence of the occupation forces was met by revolutionary counterviolence. The fall of A.D. 51 saw the first major attempt at revolt, occasioned by the murder of a Galilean pilgrim by the Samaritans in the border town of Ginea. The procurator Cumanus was able to extinguish the flame of revolt only by committing all the forces at his disposal. The Syrian governor Ummidius Quadratus and the emperor Claudius himself held all who had taken part responsible; both the procurator and the high priest were removed from office and summoned to Rome, and the commander of a Roman cohort was even executed publicly at Jerusalem on orders of the emperor on account of his excesses.[84] But all these attempts at pacification no longer bore fruit. The revolutionary guerrilla leaders with their increasingly audacious enterprises kept the people in a state of insecurity; alongside them appeared apocalyptic prophets, promising like Moses and Joshua to show their adherents once more the miracles of the desert and occupation period. The revolutionaries continued to gain ground; their goal of driving the entire nation into war with Rome was revealed more and more openly. Their irrational and utopian promise that God's miraculous help would not be displayed until the entire nation, not just a minority, entered the lists against the power of Rome gained more and more

83. Hengel, *Zeloten*, pp. 348 ff. The "famine in the reign of Claudius" around A.D. 44–48 mentioned in Acts 11:28 had devastating consequences for all of Palestine (p. 352). On Felix, see pp. 355 ff. and the verdict of Tacitus (*Hist.* v. 9): "Endowed with the mentality of a slave, he used his sovereign authority for all kinds of arbitrary brutality"; cf. *idem. Annal.* xii. 54 and Suetonius *Claudius* 28.
84. Hengel, *Zeloten*, pp. 353 ff.

adherents. The effect of such "prophecies" upon the unsophisticated can hardly be overestimated; the warning of the Synoptic apocalypses against false prophets must be understood in large measure against this background. Even when the capture of the sanctuary by the Romans was imminent, a Zealot prophesied that God was about to reveal "the sign of his redemption" in the sanctuary, inducing thousands to go up to the Temple, where they were then cut down by the invading Romans.[85] *Jesus was different*

85. Josephus *War* vi. 285–86; Hengel, *Zeloten*, pp. 248–49. On the widespread apocalyptic prophetism that raised the eschatological temper to fever pitch, see pp. 235 ff.; cf. Mark 13:6, 21–22; Matt. 24:11 ff.; Luke 21:8; John 10:8 ff.

Messianic

Expectations

It is easy to understand how the messianic apocalyptic texts of the time of Herod and the first century A.D. despite their occasionally contradictory variety, could not escape the influence of the political situation. At the very point where men ceased to hope for an earthly messianic ruler, looking instead, as in the similitudes of Ethiopian Enoch, for a heavenly Son of Man to come as redeemer and judge, hatred became especially bitter toward the "kings" and the "mighty," the "powerful," "exalted," and "rich" "who possess the earth." Over and over again the apocalyptic author depicts the judgment upon the "rulers" with total abandon:

> For the righteous and elected [they will] provide a spectacle; they will rejoice over them because the wrath of the Lord of the spirits rests upon them and his sword is drunk with their [blood].[86]

The "kings," the "mighty," and the "rich" stand in the broadest sense as representatives of the worldwide "establishment," not least the Roman overlords together with their accomplices.

---

86. Eth. En. 62:12; cf. 48:8 ff. The text is available in Kautzsch, *Apokryphen*, vol. 2, p. 272. The similitudes probably derive from the time of Herod or the first half of the first century A.D.; see Erik Sjöberg, *Der Menschensohn im äthiopischen Henochbuch* ("Skrifter utg. av Kungl. Humanistiska vetenskapssamfundet i Lund," 41 [Lund: Gleerup, 1946]), p. 39; and C. Colpe in *ThW*, vol. 8, p. 425, n. 180. On the judgment upon kings, powers, heights, and empires, see 53:5; 54:2 ff.; 55:4; 62:2–3 (Isa. 11:4), 9 ff.; 63:1 ff.; 67:7; cf. 69:27.

Possibly on the basis of historical experience, deliverance was no longer hoped for by Israel's own action in a holy war, but only through a miracle of God, through the judgment of the Son of Man, assisted by angels and bringing redemption to the "elect and righteous." It is striking to hear the voice of deep, unbridled hostility, culminating in the statement that the devout will gloat over the torments of the "rulers." The longing for eschatological justice served at the same time to satisfy the private demand for vengeance. At the same time, the similitudes show that it is incorrect to draw a one-sided distinction within Jewish apocalypticism between two types of messianic expectation, one earthly and political, the other unpolitical and transcendent. Here, too, the central act of liberation, the judgment, bears a markedly "political" stamp. The enigmatic figure of the heavenly "Son of Man" could become a kind of "antitype" of the tyrannical rulers of the earth:

> He will be a staff to the righteous and to the saints, that they may lean on him and not fall; he will be the light of the nations and the hope of those that are distressed in heart. All that dwell on the face of the earth will fall down before him. . . .
> (Eth. En. 48:4–5)

Here, too, the hope for liberation and redemption is associated with the notion of worldwide sovereignty exercised by God's deputy. It is therefore easy to understand how the Son of Man and the Davidic messiah could later totally coalesce and once more acquire martial features: the host of gentiles streaming in from the four corners of the earth is destroyed by a stream of fire from the mouth of the Son of Man-messiah.[87]

---

87. 4 Esdras 13 (Kautzsch, *Apokryphen*, vol. 2, p. 395); cf. Syr. Baruch 39–40: the destruction of the fourth empire (=Rome) and judgment upon the "final ruler," i.e., the emperor, through the messiah (Kautzsch, *Apokryphen*, vol. 2, p. 425); see Hengel, *Zeloten*, pp.

Yet another image of the messiah is provided by the Pharisaic Psalms of Solomon (Psalm 17). Here the righteous king of the line of David is ardently awaited; he is depicted as a just and sinless ruler, king of peace, and teacher. The motif of the messianic war fades into the background, and is only hinted at with reference to Isa. 11:4: "He shall destroy godless gentiles with the word of his mouth, that at the threat of him the gentiles take flight . . . (17:24–25). It is stressed, on the contrary, that after the miraculous victory, achieved without human help, he ceases to be a warlike messiah:

> His hope is not in steed, rider, and bow,
> Neither does he assemble gold or silver for war,
> And upon the multitude he does not set his hope for the day of battle.
> The Lord himself is his king, the hope of him who is strong through hope in God. (17:33–34)

Here a messiah of word and spirit is contrasted to despots after the fashion of the Hasmoneans and Herod.[88]

In the great literary apocalypses, following the prototype of the Book of Daniel, expectation of a real eschatological war took a back seat to the miraculous intervention of God and

---

308 ff. On this motif see also Rev. 19:11–21, where the Zealot spirit surfaces in the New Testament. On the rabbinic association of messiah and Son of Man, see Hermann Strack and Paul Billerbeck, *Kommentar zum Neuen Testament aus Talmud und Midrash* (München: C. H. Beck, 1922–1928), vol. 1, pp. 486, 956–57. Another line of tradition leads into Jewish mysticism; see Hugo Odeberg, *3 Enoch* (New York: Cambridge University Press, 1928).

88. The text can be found in A. Rahlfs, ed., *Septuaginta*, vol. 2, pp. 486 ff.; a German translation is available in E. Kautzsch, *Apokryphen*, vol. 2, pp. 144 ff. On the Pharisaic origin of the Psalms of Solomon, see Schalit, *König Herodes*, p. 299, n. 552, 310, 460, 464, and *passim*. This point was already made by Schürer, *History*, div. II, vol. 3, p. 21, *pace* M. de Jonge in *Novum Testamentum*, 8 (1966), pp. 134 ff.

victory without a real battle. More popular in nature and politically more effective was the hope for a true military liberator, whose military successes—like those of David—would prove him to be the redeemer sent by God. As an example, I will cite only a text from the ancient Palestinian Targum (Aramaic translation) on Gen. 49:10:

> How beautiful is the king, the messiah, who will arise from those who are of the house of Judah! He girds up his loins and goes forth and orders the battle array against his enemies and slays the kings along with their overlords, and no king or overlord can stand before him; he reddens the mountains with the blood of their slain, his clothing is dipped in blood like a winepress.[89]

The historical locus of this martial image of the messiah is probably neither the school of the scribes nor the writing desk of the apocalypticists, but the unsophisticated circles of the people, who yearned for an end to oppression and bloody vengeance for the blasphemy committed by the foreigners. This does not mean that no leading scribes supported this material messianism: A.D. 132 Rabbi Akiba openly recognized Bar Kochba as the messianic liberator and proclaimed him the "star out of Jacob" (Num. 24:17). He paid for his enthusiasm by dying a martyr's death.[90]

According to the unanimous judgment of Josephus, Tacitus, and Suetonius, such martial messianic expectations were one of the major causes of the outbreak of the Jewish War (A.D.

89. Targum Jerusalem I; see Strack-Billerbeck, *Kommentar*, vol. 4, pp. 877–78; a similar interpretation is found in Targum Jerusalem II and Targum Neofiti *ad loc.*; cf. Hengel, *Zeloten*, pp. 281 ff., 311–12. On this motif see also Rev. 14:20 and 19:17 ff.
90. Talmud Yerushalmi, Taanit 68d, 49; Strack-Billerbeck, *Kommentar*, vol. 1, p. 13; cf. Hengel, *Zeloten*, pp. 245–46. On the Bar Kochba revolt and its causes, see H. Mantel, "The Causes of the Bar Kochba Revolt," *Jewish Quarterly Review*, 58 (1968), pp. 224–42, 274–96.

66–74). According to them, the Jews had an "ambiguous oracle"—Num. 24:17 is probably meant—that they interpreted as referring to the world dominion of their nation under the messiah, while in reality it should be interpreted as referring to the emperorship of Vespasian, who, after all, had been proclaimed emperor in Palestine.[91] This argument over the interpretation of messianic prophecy shows how antithetical the Jewish expectation of deliverance was to the Roman claim to world dominion; the resulting conflict produced three catastrophes that were almost mortal to ancient Judaism. This background also helps explain how the accusation of putting forward "messianic claims" was considered a political charge *par excellence*, and almost of necessity resulted in the death penalty for the accused.

91. Josephus *War* vi. 312–13; Tacitus *Hist.* v. 13; Suetonius *Vespasian* v. 6; Hengel, *Zeloten*, pp. 243 ff.

Violence Overcome: VIII

The Message of Jesus

If one is to understand the uniqueness of Jesus' message and ministry, one must view them against the background of this acute revolutionary situation, a situation with a long history that could ultimately be traced to the historical revolution brought about by Alexander the Great.

For the unsophisticated Jewish population, it was almost entirely a history of oppressive exploitation, wars of indescribable brutality, and disappointed hopes. No other nation of the ancient world defended itself as steadfastly and bitterly against infiltration by Hellenistic civilization and oppression by the force of Roman arms as did the Jewish nation. As the three unsuccessful revolts of 66–74, 115–17, and 132–35 show,[92] this resistance almost spelled the end of the nation. The rule of Herod and his sons and the corrupt regime of the procurators—Pilate not least among them—had made the situation in Jewish Palestine so intolerable that apparently only three possibilities remained: armed revolutionary resistance, more or less opportunistic accommodation to the establishment—leaving open the possibility of mental reservations—and patient passive endurance. This last was above all the fate of the unsophisticated rural classes, the *'am hā-'āreṣ*.

It is within this dark context, which was certainly no less

92. Fuchs, *Widerstand*, pp. 20 ff.; Hengel, *Judentum*, pp. 354 ff., 555 ff.

desperate for the Jews in Palestine than all today's oppression in Latin America or elsewhere in the world, that Jesus' message and ministry must be "sketched" if we are to understand it correctly today. In a radically new way he presented an alternative allowing men to escape from these three hopeless possibilities, to break out of the vicious circle of violence and counterviolence, opportunistic complicity, and apathetic resignation, an alternative that has not lost its significance for today.

Of course I can only present this alternative in broad outline in these pages, and will concentrate on the problem of "political theology" that is especially disputed today: the question of violence.[93]

First of all, we must recognize that Jesus' appearance in public as a wandering popular preacher could be interpreted —and also, of course, misinterpreted—politically from the very beginning: by the mob in the sense that he might indeed be the messiah appointed by God to liberate Israel from the foreign yoke and bring the freedom that all longed for, and by the ruling classes, whether his sovereign Herod Antipas[94] or the leaders of the nation in Jerusalem, in the sense that his ministry to the people might serve to change the existing order by force. For this reason Herod Antipas had already had Jesus' forerunner John the Baptist executed, because he was too influential among the masses.[95] The ultimate conse-

93. Cf. also Hengel, *Was Jesus a Revolutionist?* pp. 26 ff.; Cullmann, *Jesus,* pp. 64 ff.
94. Luke 24:19–21. This passage plays a major role in the argument of Samuel G. F. Brandon, *Jesus and the Zealots* (Manchester: Manchester University Press, 1967), p. 18, n. 2, p. 19, n. 3, p. 113, n. 2. It is, of course, formulated by Luke himself. For my dispute with Brandon and the "Zealot" interpretation of Jesus and the primitive Christian community, which is once again popular, see Hengel, *Was Jesus a Revolutionist? passim.*
95. These were the grounds given by Josephus *Antiquities* xviii. 116–20 for the execution of the Baptist by Herod Antipas. Cf. Luke 13:31 ff. and Mark 3:6; 6:14 ff.

quence of this political misunderstanding was the denunciation of Jesus to Pilate by the leaders of the nation and his
dying on the cross the death of a political criminal.[96]

Not only Jesus' death but also his message contain analo-
gies to the message of the Zealots, and it is no wonder, in
view of the popular tendency for studies of Jesus to interpret
him according to the prevailing fashion of the spirit of the
age, that today men find it particularly appropriate to interpret him as a political and social revolutionist (see above,
n. 93). Like the Zealots, he proclaimed the imminence of
God's sovereignty and called on the people to repent (Mark
1:15 par.; cf. Luke 10:9, 11). At this point, however, we can
see a fundamental difference between Jesus and the zealous
revolutionists. For Jesus, the evil in the world was not to be
found primarily in the transsubjective social and political
situation, that is, in Rome as the "hegemony of wickedness,"
in the priestly aristocracy, or in the large landowners, but
rather in the evil heart of the individual.[97] The groundwork
for God's imminent sovereignty therefore cannot be laid by
the revolutionary transformation of certain political and
economic structures—the liberation of the Holy Land, the

---

96. Innumerable Jewish freedom fighters were executed by crucifixion
by the Romans in Palestine during the first century A.D.; see Hengel,
Zeloten, p. 265; Blinzler, *Prozess*, pp. 357 ff. A gruesome illustration
is provided by the discovery near Jerusalem of the skeleton of a victim of crucifixion dating from the first half of the first century A.D.;
both heels were still pierced by nails. It is still possible to reconstruct
from the skeleton the form his crucifixion took. He must have died
an infinitely painful death. Before he was taken down from the
cross, his legs were broken (John 19:32–33); when his body was
transferred to the ossuary it was anointed with oil (Mark 16:1). His
name was Johanan b. (Je)hezkel; he was 24–28 years old. Despite
his crucifixion, he was buried in a family tomb. The discoveries at the
tomb give us a general insight into the period of economic and political distress between 50 B.C. and A.D. 70. See J. Naveh and N. Haas in
Israel Exploration Journal, 20 (1967), pp. 35–59.
97. Mark 7:15 ff.; Luke 6:43 ff.; 11:20. Pauline anthropology is
already present *in nucleo* in the message of Jesus; see M. Hengel,
"Bergpredigt und Veränderung," *EvKomm*, 3 (1970), pp. 649 ff.

breaking up of large estates, and the emancipation of the slaves. Only a transformed heart is capable of new human community, of doing good. Jesus' message and conduct, both of which proclaimed the nearness of God's love, possessed such transforming power. For this very reason, Jesus—unlike the Zealots—does not present any speculative socio-political program. The coming of God's sovereignty cannot be enforced by revolutionary actions; it comes unexpectedly as God's gift, as in the parable of the seed that grows by itself (Mark 4:28): "The ground produces a crop by itself (*automatē*)." The signs of God's sovereignty, of his kingdom, do not consist in the spread of a revolutionary popular uprising, but in Jesus' preaching and his ministry of healing and helping (Luke 11:20): "If it is by the finger of God that I drive out the devils, then be sure the kingdom of God has already come among you"; or again (Luke 17:20): "The kingdom of God is among you" (in Jesus' person and message).[98]

Like the Zealots, Jesus required a radical interpretation of God's will, "tightening of the Torah." The revolutionists were concerned with the first commandment and with the prohibition of images—refusing, for example, to pick up a coin bearing the image of the emperor—as well as with the requirement that captive gentiles in the Holy Land be compelled to be circumcised. They also shared with Jesus a readiness to renounce personal property and accept martyrdom. The saying about taking up one's cross may go back to what was originally a militant Zealot saying (Mark 8.34 par.; Luke

98. On the healings of Jesus, see Hengel, *Nachfolge*, pp. 73–73, and Rudolf Pesch, *Jesu ureigene Taten?* ("Quaestiones disputatae," 52 [Freiburg: Herder, 1970]), pp. 21 ff., 140 ff. On Jesus' proclamation of the sovereignty of God, see Joachim Jeremias, *New Testament Theology. Part One: The Proclamation of Jesus* (New York: Charles Scribner's Sons, 1971), pp. 96 ff. Jeremias interprets Luke 17:20 with future meaning: "The kingdom of God will suddenly be among you." In any case there is no question of any human cooperation in paving the way for it and bringing it to pass.

14:27 par.) .[99] Jesus, however, did not take jealous zeal as his point of departure for radical interpretation of the law, but the law of love (Lev. 19:18), which he made universally applicable. For the Zealots, imitating the first "zealot" Phinehas (Numbers 25) as a model, the slaying of the godless enemy out of zeal for God's cause was a fundamental commandment, true to the rabbinic maxim: "Whoever spills the blood of one of the godless is like one who offers sacrifice."[100] Jesus, on the contrary, appealing to the Father's love for all men and radically extending the Old Testament law of love, demanded love of enemies and renunciation of violence.[101] He thus took a rigorous position against the popular morality of his age. In a sense, the law of love became to him the "law of life in the kingdom."[102] It corresponds to his requirement of unlimited readiness to forgive and renunciation of all expressions of hatred.[103] Only the experience of God's love can transform the hard heart of man, call the individual out of his bondage, and make him capable of breaching petrified

---

99. On "tightening of the Torah," see Hengel, *Zeloten*, pp. 195 ff., 201 ff., 229 ff. On "bearing one's cross," see *ibid.*, p. 266, n. 2, following A. Schlatter. For a different view, see Jeremias, *New Testament Theology*, p. 242.

100. Num. R. 21.3; Tanch. Pinchas §3, ed. Buber, 7a; Hengel, *Zeloten*, p. 164.

101. Luke 6:27–36;=Matt. 5:38–48 (Q); cf. Mark 12:28–34 parr.; Matt. 7:12; 25:31–46.

102. See Jeremias, *New Testament Theology*, pp. 211 ff.

103. Matt. 5:21 ff., 23 ff. (Luke 12:58 ff.); 6:12 ff. (Luke 11:4); 7:1 ff.; 18:21–35 (Luke 17:4); Luke 9:52–56. On hatred in ancient Judaism see above, p. 00, n. 26, and the oath at the beginning of the Manual of Discipline (1QS i. 10; Lohse, *Texte*, p. 4): ". . . to hate all the children of darkness." For further discussion, see Hengel, *Was Jesus a Revolutionist?* p. 24, n. 70. p. 38, n. 68. The "politicization" of all areas of life that is being demanded today and its associated "partisanship" carry the seeds of a menacing development: hatred is once again being represented as excusable, indeed under certain circumstances as being a "revolutionary virtue." I can still hear the voice of the teacher hammering his thesis into us at the beginning of the War: "Boys, you must learn to hate!" Similar tones can be heard in Ernesto "Che" Guevara, *Schaffen wir zwei, drei, viele Vietnams*

structures.[104] Here we come to the truly new and revolutionary element in Jesus' message, particularly in view of the centuries-long history of imperialistic violence and revolutionary counterviolence that had determined the path of his nation throughout the Hellenistic-Roman period. It is not unlikely that Jesus formulated his demand to forgive one's enemies and be ready to forgive in conscious contrast to that Zealot passion that so informed the leading intellectual and spiritual class of his nation (cf. Gal. 1:14; Phil. 3:6; Acts 22:3).

Jesus thus kept a critical distance from the political powers and authorities of his period (Matt. 11:8; Luke 13:32; 22:25). For him they are emptied of power by the nearness of God; they had become, so to speak, indifferent matters (Mark 12:13–17; cf. Matt. 17:25 ff.). Among the followers of Jesus not their laws but the order of love and service are in force. (Mark. 10:42 ff.; Luke 22:24 ff.). Thus the individual, re-

---

(Berlin, n.d.), p. 27: "Hatred as a factor in the struggle, unbending hatred of the enemy, which goads the individual beyond his natural limitations and transforms him into an effective, violent, selective, and cold mechanism of death. That is how our soldiers must be; a people without hatred cannot win over a brutal enemy." Cf. also G. von Rauch, according to *Der Spiegel*, 1970, no. 32, p. 18: "We must simply liquidate our humanity in such situations." Against such tendencies I cite the terrifying study of Jesse Glenn Gray, *Homo furens, oder braucht der Mensch den Krieg?* (Hamburg: Wegner, 1970), especially the final chapter, dealing with the future of war and his comments on "the mysterious love of violence" (p. 180) and the variations on Nietzsche's vision of "real peace, which must always rest on inner peace: while the so-called 'armed truce' that prevails today amongst all nations is the inner strife that trusts neither self nor neighbor and, half out of hatred, half out of fear, refuses to lay down weapons. Better to perish than to hate and fear, far better to perish than to make oneself hate and fear—this must finally be the highest motto of all political society!" (p. 186, quoting Friedrich Nietzsche, *Menschliches, Allzumenschliches*, 2.2, "Der Wanderer und sein Schatten," 284).
104. Luke 6:20 ff.; 7:4 ff.; 15; 18:8; 19:5; Mark 2:14; Matt. 18:12 ff.; see *EvKomm*, 3 (1970), pp. 647–51; Jeremias, *New Testament Theology*, pp. 1–121.

gardless of his situation, is "empowered" to freedom in the face of all the powers that would oppress his humanity.[105] He therefore passes harsh judgment upon unjust "worldly wealth" (Luke 16:9, 11), which in his time—as still today in lands with a feudal structure—stood in brutal contrast to the poverty of the bulk of the population. With his alternative "either God or worldly wealth" (Matt. 6:24) and his requirement to put away anxious thought (Matt. 6:25 ff.) he strikes to the roots of human existence. But even these demands are not based on some binding "social program" but on the offer of unconditional trust in the goodness of the Father. Whoever trusts more in worldly wealth falls into *sin of compromise* idolatry and is thus subject to God's judgment. Jesus' strong emphasis on this ultimate responsibility of man before his creator links him with the call to repentance of his forerunner, John the Baptist, and the proclamation of the Old Testament prophets (Luke 3:7–14 par.; 7:24 par.; Matt. 21:31 ff.). None of his contemporaries criticized more sharply *yet He did not encourage them to seek wealth* than he the complacent, self-satisfied Babbitts that sought the meaning of life primarily in the acquisition of riches. His message was thus socially and politically explosive, a trait that has reappeared repeatedly throughout its history, down to L. Ragaz and Leo Tolstoy.[106] If it were not so, it would be almost impossible to understand why the lower classes came

105. On Mark 12:13–17, see Hengel, *Zeloten*, pp. 198 ff., and *idem, Was Jesus a Revolutionist?* pp. 33–35, p. 33, n. 91.
106. Mark 10:17–31 parr.; Mark 12:40–44; Luke 6:24–25; 12:13–21; 16:19–31; cf. Matt. 25:41 ff.; James 2:1–7. Throughout the course of church history down to the world of today Jesus' message has acted as the leaven of social criticism. It is significant that in the process the apocalyptic Jewish ideas of the kingdom of God upon earth have constantly taken shape again. The result has frequently been chiliastic movements, especially in regions with a feudal social structure and in missionary territory, from the Hussites to the Taiping revolt in China and the cargo cult in Melanesia. See Sylvia Lettice Thrupp, *Millennial Dreams in Action* (New York: Schocken Books, 1970). With regard to this element of "social criticism" in Jesus' message, we can

to him in such droves; for this very reason he aroused the suspicions and fears of the national leaders, of Herod Antipas in Galilee and the Sanhedrin at Jerusalem. This appeal to the *'am hā-'āreṣ*, the uneducated people "who do not know the law" and are therefore accused,[107] he may also share with the revolutionists. But he never allowed this openness to the religiously and socially déclassé, despised by the upper classes, to be restricted by political barriers. He addressed himself not

---

still hear the challenging significance of the ironic questions of the twenty-four-year-old Karl Marx (*Rheinische Zeitung*, 14 July 1842) concerning the betrayal of Jesus' message by the bourgeoisie of the Restoration (*Karl Marx—Friedrich Engels, Historische-kritische Gesamtausgabe* [Frankfurt: Marx-Engels Archiv, 1927–   ], 1. Abt., I. 1, pp. 246 ff.). Of course he was not arguing *for* a politicization of the Christian faith, but rather *against* it in its traditional form of an alliance between throne and altar; in other words, he supported a clear distinction between the two "kingdoms": "Are not the majority of your trials, the majority of your civil laws, concerned with property? But it has been told you that your treasures are not of this world. Or if you appeal to the principle of rendering to Caesar what is Caesar's and to God what is God's, then consider not only golden mammon but at least free reason as the Caesar of this world, and let us call the 'action of free reason' the Caesar of this world." It is true—as the history of modern philosophy shows—that when "values" are concerned, i.e., in the realm of ethics and politics, the "action of free reason" cannot be carried out as "uniformly" as in mathematics. History also teaches that when a dogma of social ethics is elevated to the status of a political absolute on the basis of an appeal to reason, this "Caesar" can under certain circumstances turn into an inhuman tyrant. As an example of the dichotomy possible within "free reason," I cite only the contradictory political programs of Herbert Marcuse and Karl Popper in the *Süddeutsche Zeitung* of January 16/17, 1971. The problem is that although *both* have good "grounds of reason" on their side, they arrive at contradictory conclusions. On the whole, the closing words of Popper appear more convincing to me: "Through violence it is very easy to destroy men. What is necessary is to work for a more rational society, in which conflicts are increasingly worked out on a rational basis. I say 'more rational'! There is in fact no such thing as a rational society, but there is one that is more rational than existing society, and we must therefore strive to achieve it. That is a realistic challenge, not a utopia."

107. John 7:49; cf. Strack-Billerbeck, *Kommentar*, vol. 2, pp. 494–519, where the utter contempt of the Pharisees for the "people of the land" is cited. The term finally became an opprobrious epithet of any Jew who was not a Pharisee.

He did not promise riches here,

only to the totally "useless," the poorest of the poor, the sick —lepers, for instance[108]—but also to the "traitors to the nation" and "exploiters," the universally hated tax collectors. To these very men he gave his love and companionship, without regard for the universal offense that must be given by such provocation, political as well as social. Today one would say that he consorted with "enemies of the people." It was no less offensive that he could represent the "popular enemy," the Samaritan, as a model in contrast to the hereditary Jewish aristocracy, the priest and Levite.[109] In other words, Jesus' message could not be pigeonholed in any of the contemporary religious or political schemata; his critical attitude touched in fundamental terms all the contemporary Jewish "parties" in Palestine. His hostility toward the priestly aristocracy of the Sadducees is shown, for instance, by his prophetical, symbolic

108. Cf. also Mark 1:40 ff. par.; 14:3 par.; Matt. 10:8; 11:5 par.; Luke 17:12 ff. Even if a healing narrative like Luke 17:12 ff. contains legendary features, there can be no doubt of the fact that Jesus addressed himself to lepers, *pace* Pesch, *Jesu ureigene Taten,* pp. 35 ff., 135. If Jesus expressed his concern for the sick at all, he certainly included the lepers, who were really the most wretched of the wretched on account of the rigorous restrictions of Leviticus 13—14 (13:45–46). According to Josephus (*Antiquities* iii. 264; cf. *Contra Apionem* i. 281), a leper was tantamount to a dead man. Here Pesch's exegesis loses its historical moorings, because it does not take sufficient account of the sociological background. It is also significant that in the rabbinic view this very disease was considered a deserved punishment, sent by God for open or secret sins: see *EvKomm,* 3 (1970), p. 650 and Strack-Billerbeck, *Kommentar,* vol. 1, pp. 228–29; vol. 2, pp. 136–37, 194 ff.; vol. 3, pp. 767, 794; vol. 4, pp. 745 ff. Furthermore, the permanent ritual uncleanness associated with leprosy placed the sufferer in total isolation. For this reason association with and probably also healing of individuals considered lepers must be counted among Jesus' *ipsissima facta* if his ministry is to be presented in anything like reasonable terms against its contemporary background.

109. Mark 2:14 ff. parr.; Matt. 11:19 par.; 21:31; Luke 18:8 ff.; 19:1–10; see O. Michel in *ThW,* vol. 8, pp. 103 ff.; Jeremias, *New Testament Theology,* pp. 109 ff. On the Samaritans, see Hengel, *Was Jesus a Revolutionist?* p. 25, n. 71.

act of cleansing the Temple, which must by no means be reinterpreted as an armed attack on the Temple—it was rather an exemplary demonstration against the misuse of the sanctuary to enrich the leading priestly families.[110] Their response—shortly thereafter—was to have the Jewish police arrest Jesus in Gethsemane and deliver him to the Romans as an alleged political criminal. The pericope of the tribute money (see above, n. 105) demonstrates how the extreme right, the Herodians, could plot against Jesus with the left-wing Pharisees because they *both* considered him highly embarrassing (cf. Mark 3:6). But even to the revolutionary Zealots Jesus appeared hardly less dangerous than to the establishment, for: (1) he had great influence among the simple rural population of Galilee, in other words, their primary source of recruits; and (2) his demand for love of enemies and renunciation of violence was in extreme opposition to their ideal of revolutionary zeal. They therefore necessarily perceived his message as a direct threat. He appeared simultaneously as a "competitor" and a "traitor." This means that both the extreme right and the left of Jesus' period rejected him as an intolerable provocation, and his death was undoubtedly welcomed by both wings.

His most extreme provocation was his linking of his message of unconditional love and readiness to forgive, based on the nearness of God, with a messianic claim. Decision with respect to his message was a matter of life and death, acceptance into the kingdom of God's sovereignty or exclusion from it.[111] Without going into further detail on the almost impenetrable problem of Jesus' claim to be sent by

110. Mark 11:15 ff. parrs.; cf. John 2:14 ff.; see Hengel, *Zeloten*, p. 221; *idem, Was Jesus a Revolutionist?* pp. 15–18; p. 16, nn. 53–54; p. 17, nn. 55–56.
111. Matt. 11:5; Mark 8:38 parr.; Luke 12:8 par.; 13:28; Matt. 25:14–30 (= Luke 19:12–27); and elsewhere. See Jeremias, *New Testa-*

God and his own self-awareness, I should like to stress that
he unambiguously associated his own person and commission
with the enigmatic figure of the coming heavenly "[Son of]
Man."[112] He put forward his claim to speak with greater
authority than Moses or the prophets;[113] in other words, he
made his appearance in order to announce the final, ultimate
"revelation of God," the true will of the Father, and at the
same time his unconditional love for all lost souls. He could
therefore term his forerunner, the Baptist, the "greatest among
those born of woman," exceeding the measure of the

---

ment Theology, pp. 122 ff., 142 ff., 151 ff. Jesus' preaching of repentance is of course totally in the context of the offer of "unrestricted
grace," pp. 173 ff. He therefore did not found a self-contained remnant
community like that of the Essenes; he was concerned instead to
make God's nearness known to the entire nation; see Hengel, *Nachfolge*, pp. 67, 76 ff.
112. I would only state that William Wrede, *Das Messiasgeheimnis in
den Evangelien* (3rd ed.; Göttingen: Vandenhoeck & Ruprecht, 1963),
with his thesis of a totally unmessianic Jesus has led a major portion
of German New Testament studies along a false trail, for this approach renders incomprehensible the sudden appearance of the post-
Easter Son of Man Christology and the total restriction of the title
"Son of Man" to Jesus' statements about himself. In order to invali-
date the clear statements of the Gospels, scholarship has had to adopt
the most daring hypotheses. The dilemma is made even worse by the
suggestion of P. Vielhauer (*Aufsätze zum Neuen Testament*, 1965,
pp. 52 ff., 92 ff.) that the idea of God's kingdom is traditio-histori-
cally irreconcilable with messianic titles, and that for this reason all
the Son of Man passages in the Gospels, even those considered
authentic by Wrede and Bultmann, dealing with the coming Son of
Man are later products of the Christian community. This makes the
development of Christology totally inexplicable. The hypothesis is
already contradicted by Daniel 7 and Psalms of Solomon 17:3, 21, 32,
34, and 46; cf. M. de Jonge in *Novum Testamentum*, 8 (1966), p. 136,
as well as by the eleventh and fourteenth of the Eighteen Benedic-
tions; now cf. also 11QMelch, lines 16 and 18 (see above, n. 74). One
can only express astonishment that this hypothesis found so many
adherents. The support is clearly based less on historical considerations than on theological desiderata. For a counterargument, see C.
Colpe in *ThW*, vol. 8, pp. 443–46 and n. 291; cf. Jeremias, *New Testament Theology*, pp. 257 ff., where the problem is clearly summarized.
113. Matt. 5:21 ff.; 11:41 par.; Luke 10:24 par.; cf. Jeremias, *New
Testament Theology*, pp. 82 ff., and, on the "emphatic *egō*," pp. 250 ff.

prophets.[114] The characterization of Jesus as "rabbi and prophet," developed by liberal scholarship and adopted by Rudolf Bultmann and some of his pupils, is totally inadequate to express this messianic claim. Only on this basis can one understand why Jesus not only proclaimed the fulfillment of the Old Testament promises—as in the Beatitudes and his reply to the Baptist[115]—but at the same time called the Torah itself into question, the Torah that to the Jew was identical with the law of the world, indeed with the cosmic order of the universe, that guaranteed Israel's election and right to dominion, and at the same time legitimized Israel's struggle for political and social self-assertion and, what is more, its eschatological victory over the nations.[116]

Jesus' messianic claim represented a radical break with these traditional features of Jewish messianic expectation; he thus gave his message an unlimited universality that broke down all barriers of social privilege, nationality, and race, even though his ministry was to all intents and purposes limited to Palestinian Jews. From the perspective of traditional Judaism he could appear, so to speak, as an "anti-messiah," and the Jewish tradition of the Toledot Jeshu so terms him occasionally.[117]

Jesus' attack upon the law, carried on consistently by Paul, still challenges us today: what is at stake is also abolition of what the law compels, self-vindication and self-assertion at any price, aggressive retaliation, and self-justification of

114. Matt. 11:9, 11 (= Luke 7:26, 28); cf. Matt. 11:12 (= Luke 16:16); see Jeremias, *New Testament Theology*, pp. 46 ff.
115. Hengel, *Nachfolge*, pp. 41 ff., 46 ff., 70 ff., 74 ff.; cf. Jeremias, *New Testament Theology*, pp. 76 ff. Isa. 61:1 ff. is in the background.
116. Hengel, *Judentum*, pp. 289 ff., 307 ff.
117. Samuel Krauss, *Das Leben Jesu nach jüdischen Quellen* (Berlin: Calvary, 1902); cf. W. Horbury, "The Trial of Jesus in Jewish Tradition," in *The Trial of Jesus; Cambridge Studies in Honour of C. F. D. Moule,* ed. Ernst Bammel ("Studies in Biblical Theology," 2nd ser., 13 [Naperville: Allenson, 1970]), pp. 103–21.

violence and glorification of ruthless success. These manifold inner laws of the life struggle and use of violence Jesus opposes as one who summons men to freedom,[118] a freedom of love and goodness informed by the love of the Father, by unconditional openness and trust—even in the face of hate and distrust—and, finally, by freedom to suffer and to sacrifice, upon a way that Jesus himself followed to the bitter end. The injustice and suffering in Palestine two thousand years ago was certainly no less than the suffering in our world today. The revolutionary prescriptions of our time for the overcoming of such injustice and suffering are likewise not always so very different from those proposed then. The idea that the present-day situation has become intolerable, so that

118. In Ernst Käsemann's impassioned polemic *Der Ruf der Freiheit* (3rd ed.; Tübingen: Mohr, 1968), the chapter "Was Jesus a 'liberal'?" (pp. 16–41) is especially significant. In Jesus, according to Käsemann, we really hear "the voice of religious enlightenment." He was, thus, far ahead of his time and indeed of our time, which speaks so glibly of enlightenment and stands in such desperate need of true "enlightenment." In his criticism of the Torah and the cult as well as in the law of love Jesus brings faith and reason together (pp. 40–41). This certainly does not exhaust the meaning of Jesus' ministry, but it is a significant component for our time. The problem is that at the very point where the appeal to reason is constantly made we are so terribly "unreasonable," refusing to "listen to reason" and hear what the moment demands, all too frequently following instead our atavistic emotions (see above, n. 103, and below, n. 120). This *agapē*, the only truly rational love for one's neighbor, that Jesus demands of us proves now and then to be too much for us, because we do not know what true freedom is, freedom from ourselves. That is also the reason why Jesus did not require love "on the strength of any human ideal" that is freely available to mankind, "but connected it directly with the beginning of God's reign on earth, and he made it his aim that that newly inaugurated reign of God should be accepted and extended . . . . He was liberal in a different way from all other people . . . . He was unique in that he remained, lived and died, acted and spoke, in the freedom of being a child of God. *The freedom of God's children, who were lost but are now reconciled and recalled,* is his revelation, his glory, gift, and claim. Since him and through him the freedom of God's children has been the true symbol of the gospel and the final criterion for all who call themselves Christians . . . ." (pp. 40–41; my emphasis).

revolutionary violence has become justified, even necessary, was widespread then as now—and it was not the most wicked who were proclaiming this idea. Those who justify violence today do not see that they are starting a vicious circle from which they can scarcely escape, and which—as is shown by the history of the revolutions in Palestine in the time of Jesus and in Europe during the past two hundred years—will either corrupt them through abuse of their new-found power or, if they seek to preserve their "humanity," drive them into opposition and finally liquidate them as alleged "counter-revolutionaries."

In the midst of an outwardly hopeless situation, Jesus taught his group of followers how to break out of this vicious circle; until the age of Constantine, the early church adhered unflinchingly to this refusal to use violence.[119] It is part of the critical power of the gospel that this summons to freedom —which also means freedom from the inner law of violence[120]

---

119. See the excellent summary of Roland H. Bainton, "Die frühe Kirche und der Krieg" (1946) in *Das frühe Christentum und der römische Staat*, ed. Richard Klein ("Wege der Forschung," 267 [Darmstadt: Wissenschaftliche Buchgesellschaft, 1971]), pp. 187–216.
120. On the problem of the use of violence, the subject of much discussion today in social ethics, see Hengel, *Was Jesus a Revolutionist?* pp. 30–33, nn. 85–88; T. Rendtorff, "Wo sich die Geister scheiden," *EvKomm*, 2 (1969), pp. 147–48; R. Strunk, "Aspekte des Gewaltproblems im Kontext einer Theologie der Revolution," in Ernst Feil and Rudolf Weth, eds., *Diskussion zur "Theologie der Revolution"* (München: Kaiser, 1969), pp. 270–90. This problem is especially acute today in the context of the program against racism; see the discussions in *EvKomm*, 3 (1970) under the entry *"Gewalt, Gewaltlosigkeit"* on page x of the index; see also Arend Theodor van Leeuwen, *Revolution als Hoffnung—Strategie des sozialen Wandels* (Stuttgart: Kreuz, 1970), pp. 50 ff., 161 ff., and Johannes Degen, *Das Problem der Gewalt* ("Konkretionen," 9 [Hamburg: Furche, 1970]). Both books disappoint the reader, since their "theological reflection" is extremely weak and their information about political structures very biased. Degen's book, for example, culminates in the fundamental demand for ideological "partisanship" (pp. 129–30). A completely different tack is taken by the fine pastoral study of Roger Schutz, *Die Gewalt der Friedfertigen* (Gütersloh: Mohn, 1970); suggestive beginnings will be found in Theodor Ebert, *Gewaltfreier Aufstand*

—is still heard today, is in fact once again being heard more clearly. Fundamentally, today's dispute over the possibility and proper form of a "political theology" is concerned with the old conflict between law and gospel, between the self-justification of the man who seeks his salvation in the law and allows his means to be justified through the law, and the justification of the godless man who is set free to enjoy his true humanity through the unmerited love of God.[121] Reflection on the message of Jesus against the background of the unimaginable brutality and injustice of his age could help us today better to understand the gospel, that is, Jesus' summons to freedom, and to act accordingly.

("Sozialwissenschaft in Theorie und Praxis" [Freiburg i. Br.: Rombach, 1968]), who examines the possibility of "nonviolent" change through which opponents are not liquidated but persuaded.
121. E. Grässer, "Die politische Herausforderung an die biblische Theologie," *EvTh*, 30 (1970), pp. 228–54 (246–47).

The Way of the   IX

First Christians

Finally, let us inquire into the attitude of the primitive Christian community. It neither went the easy way of joining the Zealot liberation movement nor glorified Jesus as a martyr for the cause of Israelite nationalism, slain by the Romans and leaders of the nation.[122] Instead, the appearances of the risen Lord gave the disciples a missionary task, already sketched by Jesus in principle: first as a responsibility toward their own people, then, a few years later in Paul's vision of Christ, as a mission to all nations and peoples. The resurrection visions were thus not an end in themselves, but embodied this very missionary commission.[123] The means to carry out this task also remained the same as those used by Jesus: the

---

122. Above all Samuel G. F. Brandon, *The Fall of Jerusalem and the Christian Church* (London: SPCK, 1951); *Jesus and the Zealots* (Manchester: Manchester University Press, 1967); *The Trial of Jesus of Nazareth* (London: Batsford, 1968), who tries to depict not only Jesus but also the primitive Christian community in Jerusalem as a movement very near to Zealotism; in the course of his argument he often does violence to his sources. See my review in *Journal of Semitic Studies*, 14 (1969), pp. 231–40; Hengel, *Was Jesus a Revolutionist? passim; idem, Zeloten*, pp. 306–307. It was only logical for the Jerusalem community to flee to the Hellenistic city of Pella in Transjordan before the outbreak of the Jewish War (Eusebius *Ecclesiastical History* iii. 5. 3) and for the pseudomessiah Bar Kochba later to persecute the Christians in Palestine (Justin *Apology* i. 31. 6; = Eusebius *Ecclesiastical History* iv. 8. 4).

123. See Heinrich Kasting, *Die Anfänge der urchristlichen Mission* ("Beiträge zur evangelischen Theologie," 55 [München: Kaiser, 1969]), pp. 35–81; cf. M. Hengel in *New Testament Studies*, 17 (1970/71).

spoken word and the helping deed. The fundamental renunciation of violence was implicit. The hope for eschatological
world dominion on the part of Israel, which manifested itself,
for instance, in the prophetic and apocalyptic notion of the
gentile pilgrimage, a notion that at first continued to play a
role within the Palestinian community, disappeared. In its
place there arose relatively quickly the demand for an active
mission among all nations, without first circumcising the
gentiles in order to make them proselytes, that is, Jews. The
revolutionary significance of this decision, which overcame
the gulf between Jew and gentile that had previously determined Jewish history in its entirety, can hardly be measured.
A centuries-old, insurmountable wall of mutual mistrust and
hatred was broken down.[124] That this should lead to occa-
sional difficulties is only natural. It was therefore all the more
significant that they were overcome and the early church was
not torn asunder. The decision of the Jerusalem community
at the so-called Apostolic Council some eighteen years after
the crucifixion of Jesus (A.D. 48) to legitimize this missionary
work (Gal. 2:1–10; Acts 15) bears witness to an astounding
magnanimity that can hardly be explained on other grounds
than the sense of obligation felt even by the "pillars" at
Jerusalem (Gal. 2:9) to follow the intent of Jesus' message.
For this bold step necessarily meant defamation for them and
persecution by the Jewish majority in Palestine (1 Thes.
2:14 ff.). Given this background, it is no accident that Paul
could call his missionary message, directed to the entire
world, "the word of reconciliation" (*logos tēs katallagēs*).
This reconciliation was not, of course, any short-circuited
"reconciliation" in the sense of "human brotherhood," but
had reference to the reconciliation of hostile men with God

124. Cf. also the later reflection on this step in Eph. 2:11–19 and
the cosmic reconciliation of the world in the hymn in Col. 1:19–20.

through the death of Jesus.[125] This concept of "reconcilia-tion," which is fundamental to Paul, must be understood at least in part against the background of the ideology of sovereignty in the ancient world. Plutarch called Alexander the "universal author of peace and reconciler of the world," who "brings all men together in unity by words and force of violence." In similar fashion, Horace's *Carmen saeculare* and the fourth *Eclogue* of Virgil sang the praises of Augustus as bringer of reconciliation to the world, while in the Jewish *Sybilline Oracles* God himself reconciles opposites and inaugurates a kingdom of peace following his court of judg-ment.[126] According to Paul, on the contrary, men experience God's reconciling love in the death and resurrection of Jesus (Rom. 5:6–11), and being thus reconciled receive the free-dom to break down social and national barriers. In Gal. 3:28 Paul gives this idea truly revolutionary expression: "There is no such thing as Jew and Greek, slave and freeman, male and female; for you are all one person in Christ Jesus."

Despite all the persecution and defamation to which he was exposed (2 Cor. 11:23 ff.), Paul was able to affirm the *Pax Romana* because it provided a kind of "liberated zone" for the missionary proclamation of the gospel. He shared this relatively positive attitude toward the Roman state with the majority of Diaspora Judaism, of which he was himself a product. It is against this background that we must read

125. 2 Cor. 5:17–21. Such reconciliation brings about a "new crea-tion" (*kainē ktisis*); cf. M. Hengel in *Theologie und Kirche; Reiche-nau Gespräch* (Stuttgart, 1967), pp. 69–89; P. Stuhlmacher, "Erwäg-ungen zum ontologischen Charakter der KAINE KTISIS bei Paulus," *EvTh*, 27 (1967), pp. 1–35; and the same author's fine discussion of the relationship between the idea of peace and reconciliation in the New Testament, "Der Begriff des Friedens im Neuen Testament und seine Konsequenzen," in *Historische Beiträge zur Friedensforschung*, ed. W. Huber ("Studien zur Friedensforschung," 4 [Stuttgart: Klett, 1970]), pp. 21–69 (33 ff., 37 ff.).
126. *De Alex. fort. aut. virt.* 6 (329 c); Sib. iii. 367 ff., 741 ff., 785 ff.; cf. ii. 319 ff.

Rom. 13:1–7; under no circumstances should this passage be misunderstood as an eternally valid prescription for an attitude of reverence toward the state. Probably Paul formulated this excursus with one eye on the special situation of the Christian community of Rome, only a few years after Claudius's banishment of the Christians (Suetonius *Claudius* xxv. 3). This much-misunderstood and much-abused text is corrected by Acts 5:29 as well as by Revelation 13 with its vision of the demonic power of the totalitarian state. One must also not overlook the setting of Rom. 13:1–7: it is set within a framework expounding the law of love (12:17–21 and 13:8–10), in which for Paul—as for Jesus—the law is summed up, transforming itself radically into promise, that is, gospel.[127] Christian love, *agapē*, defines the limit of the power exercised by the state and society; through love the believer gains the liberty to "use good to defeat evil" (Rom. 12:21). As 1 Peter, the Pastorals, and later the apologists show, early Christianity firmly maintained this attitude, informed by *agapē*, toward the world in which it found itself, despite the persecutions on the part of the Roman state beginning with Nero and Domitian.[128] From time to time, as in Revelation, which was composed in a situation of acute persecution, a kind of "Zealot raid" undoubtedly occurred. But even here the community persevered in suffering and renounced all violent means of aid: "This is where the

127. *EvKomm*, 3 (1970), p. 650: "Jesus' demand has 'the nature of a promise,' because at the very point where it demands the seemingly impossible, it leads man to his true nature—the *imago dei*. Not 'God's' but 'man's' being is in the process of 'becoming.'" On Romans 13 and the problem of the state in the New Testament, see now W. Schrage, *Die Christen und der Staat nach dem Neuen Testament* (1970), pp. 50 ff. Cf. also M. Dibelius, "Rom und die Christen im ersten Jahrhundert," in *Das frühe Christentum und der römische Staat*, ed. Richard Klein ("Wege der Forschung," 267 [Darmstadt: Wissenschaftliche Buchgesellschaft, 1971]), pp. 47–105 (51 ff.).
128. Schrage, *Christen*, pp. 63 ff.; Dibelius, "Rom," pp. 61 ff.

patience and faithfulness of God's people have their place"
(Rev. 13:10).[129] Finally, Justin may speak as a representative
of the second-century witnesses: "We who were full of war,
mutual slaughter, and depravity of all sorts have throughout
the world exchanged our weapons—swords for plowshares
and spears for pruning-hooks." In his apology to the emperor
Antoninus Pius he stresses the necessary connection between
renunciation of violence and readiness to suffer: "We who
once killed each other have now not only renounced war
against our enemies, but, so as not to lie or deceive our
judges, we gladly die for the confession of Christ."[130] Between
A.D. 163 and 167, before the Roman city prefect Junius Rusti-
cus, he sealed the truth of these words with his own life.

Today, some eighteen hundred years later, we are being
asked whether, renouncing the message of Jesus, we wish to
return to those atavistic ideologies that glorify violence in
the name of a pseudoreligion. For the Christian to whom the
origin of his faith still means something, it is salutary to look
back on this period. There is a danger confronting any
"political theology" that ignores the monstrous extent of
oppression and exploitation, violence and counterviolence in
Jewish Palestine in the time of Jesus and refuses at the same
time to take seriously the radically different response of Jesus
and the early Christians to this hopeless situation: the danger
of giving up its claim to be "political theology" and turning
instead into mere "political theory" or "action."

129. Dibelius, "Rom," pp. 94 ff.
130. *Dialogue with Trypho* cx. 3; *Apology* xxxix. 2; see Bainton,
"Frühe Kirche," p. 195.

Five Theses on the   X
Problem of Violence

(1) Jesus' liberating message of love without restriction includes also renunciation of the violence that destroys one's fellow man physically or mentally. Violence has irreparable consequences for the individual and for society.

(2) Called by Christ to freedom from this destructive violence, the Christian knows that he faces a conflict that—humanly speaking—is insoluble. For the forms of human society in which he finds himself claim that, for their own protection and in order to preserve or establish freedom and justice, they cannot renounce the use of such destructive violence in cases of necessity, such as always arise. All that matters, according to this claim, is that the use of violence be "appropriate."

(3) For the Christian, appeal to such "necessity" can never "justify" such violence; its use—even in self-defense—brings guilt upon the individual and upon society. The Christian knows that he cannot live in this world without now and then incurring guilt; but for this very reason he has no use for "self-justification" and palliation when he believes that he or the society of which he is a part cannot, for the sake of justice, forgo taking human life. He must rather examine himself to see whether what is at work here—in himself above all—is not suppressed aggression, envy, the instinct of vengeance, lack of readiness to suffer, and the impatience that springs from unbelief. He cannot be satisfied with the

judicious balancing of violence and counterviolence, and the knowledge that violence is "appropriate."

(4) These considerations hold true all the more today, when the forces that—for whatever reasons—glorify violence, awaken aggressive instincts, even exploit them politically and commercially, are growing ever more powerful. The signs are terrifyingly manifold. These include not only the wars in Vietnam, in the Near East, in southern Sudan, East Pakistan, etc., but also the constant abuse of positions of political and economic power, the uncontrolled power of the "secret police" in many countries, the manipulated "voice of the people" calling for the death penalty; they include public executions, the glorification of assassinations, the taking of hostages and throwing of bombs, all the barbaric forms of punishment executed upon political opponents; they include commitment to mental hospitals, use of torture to extract statements, and the manifold forms of censorship and manipulation of information on the part of mass media. It is striking to observe that this growing abuse of violence is by no means associated with specific political creeds, but can in fact threaten us under all political systems, although "totalitarian" systems are especially susceptible because they lack democratic controls. It is also striking to observe that in present-day political polarization the various groups—including the theologians—prefer to see the mote in the other man's eye.

(5) The goal of the Christian for whom Jesus' summons to freedom still has any meaning must be to reduce and restrict such violence, especially when it is disguised as "self-defense." This means that he is ready to oppose all glorification and justification of violence and to reveal its hidden abuse. This critical task concerns first and foremost the "established forces of violence," but by no means excludes "revolutionary counterviolence." Obviously this "prophetic"

task must not be undertaken with Pharisaic self-righteousness, but in a spirit of self-criticism. For it could be that we ourselves are profiting from the system of violence that we indict; neither is it our purpose to damn the other man, but to persuade him and thus to help him. This "prophetic" task also means a long "learning process," the consequence of which will be that the Christians involved, who always represent only a minority, are attacked from different fronts simultaneously as "revolutionaries" and as "reactionaries." Such attacks should confirm them that the way they are taking is the right way. On this point the following of Jesus is identical with reason, not as a legal compulsion that kills and damns but as a summons to the freedom that gives life.